THE CONCEPT OF GRACE

THE CONCEPT OF GRACE

*Essays on the Way of Divine Love
in Human Life*

PHILIP S. WATSON

WIPF & STOCK · Eugene, Oregon

Wipf and Stock Publishers
199 W 8th Ave, Suite 3
Eugene, OR 97401

The Concept of Grace
Essays on the Way of Divine Love in Human Life
By Watson, Philip S.
Copyright©1959 Methodist Publishing - Epworth Press
ISBN 13: 978-1-4982-0498-9
Publication date 9/11/2014
Previously published by Epworth Press, 1959

Every effort has been made to trace the current copyright
owner of this publication but without success. If you have any
information or interest in the copyright, please contact the publishers.

Preface

CHRISTIANITY is pre-eminently a religion of grace. Even where the word 'grace' is not used, the idea of grace in other terms holds a quite central place in all genuine Christianity. If that idea becomes weakened or displaced, then whether the word 'grace' is used or not, Christianity inevitably loses something of its essential character. So much is this the case, that in any attempt to explain the meaning of grace, it is almost necessary to give an account, at least in outline, of the entire Christian faith. The Christian faith, however, has had a history. It has not remained unchangeably the same at all times and in all places. It has appeared in very different guises in the different environments of life and thought into which it has entered. Hence the concept of grace also has a history. The place and significance attributed to it have not always and everywhere been precisely the same. Even among its greatest exponents there have been differences of emphasis and point of view; and among their followers there have been different degrees of comprehension of their teaching.

Just as a coin that is in constant use quickly becomes tarnished, and in time grows worn and thin, so the original signification of a word is often obscured; and just as money values change with changing circumstances, so the meanings of words can change. A penny once meant to an Englishman a silver coin, the two-hundred-and-fortieth part of a pound weight of silver—the 'pound sterling'. It came to mean a coin made of copper and weighing an ounce, then a lighter one of bronze—which is still often called a 'copper'. The silver penny declined progressively in weight and value during the centuries when it was in use, and the bronze penny, as we know only too well, no longer has the purchasing power either of the copper or of its own original self. Yet a penny is still legal tender, and there are still two hundred and forty pence to the pound. Moreover, if currency can suffer 'inflation' and a decline in purchasing power, it can also undergo 'deflation' and recover lost value; and it can even be 'reformed', as happened in Western Germany a few years ago, to the great advantage of the national economy.

Now something similar to all this can be said both of words in general, and not least of words belonging to the theological vocabulary, such as 'grace'. In the New Testament the word 'grace', which was current already in classical and Hellenistic Greek, received a great enrichment of meaning. In the course of Christian history this meaning has not infrequently been obscured and even debased, though it has never been wholly lost. At the Reformation it was largely rediscovered; in the Evangelical Revival it was reaffirmed, though not without some differences of emphasis; and today, through the revival of biblical theology, it is again coming into its own.

The following chapters are all concerned in one way or another with the understanding of the idea of grace, if not always directly with the word 'grace' itself. The first of them examines the use of the term by St Paul, who must be regarded as the classic exponent of its Christian meaning. The next three are intended as illustrating the variety of ways in which the idea of grace finds expression in New Testament Christianity. The fifth seeks to show how essentially the same idea is embodied in the credal formulations of the Early Church—and how it is distorted in some more recent dogmatic pronouncements. The sixth reviews the rise and controversial progress of a specific doctrine of grace, describing its main features as they appear in the work of the Fathers, the Schoolmen and the Reformers. Then in the concluding chapter, in which traditional theological language is as far as possible discarded, an attempt is made to consider how far the facts of our human experience justify us in speaking of the reality of grace.

These chapters owe their existence together in the present volume largely to the generous reception given at the Fellowship of the Kingdom Conference of 1954 to an address by their author on the meaning of grace. Pressure of other duties has prevented the fulfilment of a promise to turn that address into a book, and what is offered here is rather a selection of essays bearing on the same theme. My thanks are due to the Editor of *The Expository Times* for permission to use in Chapters 3 and 4 articles written (in 1940 and 1950 respectively) at his request, and to the Editor of *The London Quarterly and Holborn Review* for permission to use in Chapter 2 an article published in 1948. The remaining chapters consist of hitherto unpublished lectures and addresses. I am grateful to those who by their invitations to write or speak gave me the incentive to prepare these essays, and particularly to the brethren of 'F.K.', from whose kindness I have perhaps taken too much courage.

PHILIP S. WATSON

WESLEY HOUSE
CAMBRIDGE

Contents

	PREFACE	5
I	ST PAUL'S CONCEPTION OF GRACE	11
II	BAPTISM AS A MEANS OF GRACE .	18
III	JUSTIFICATION AS A WORK OF GRACE	31
IV	THE HOLY SPIRIT OF GRACE . .	44
V	DOGMA AS AN AFFIRMATION OF GRACE	55
	1 THE PROBLEM OF DOGMA	55
	2 THE FORMAL CHARACTER OF DOGMA . .	59
	3 THE ESSENTIAL CONTENT OF DOGMA .	63
	4 THE VALIDITY OF DOGMA . . .	69
VI	DEVELOPMENTS OF THE DOCTRINE OF GRACE	75
	1 GRACE AS AN INFUSED POWER . . .	75
	2 GRACE CONTRASTED WITH NATURE . .	77
	3 GRACE COMBINED WITH MERIT . . .	83
	4 GRACE MEDIATED SACRAMENTALLY . .	87
	5 GRACE AND FREE WILL	95

VII	THE REALITY OF GRACE	.	.	.	102
1	GRACE IN CREATION	.	.	.	102
2	GRACE IN CHRIST .	.	.	.	106
3	GRACE IN THE CHURCH .	.	.	.	111

ONE

St Paul's Conception of Grace

THE FIRST great exponent of grace in the Christian sense of the term is St Paul. The word occurs more frequently and characteristically in his writings than anywhere else in the New Testament, and the richness of specifically Christian content that it possesses is primarily due to him. Not that St Paul was the originator either of the word or the idea of grace. The idea is already present in the life and teaching of Jesus as He is portrayed in the Synoptic Gospels,[1] and it is also to be found in various forms in the Old Testament.[2] The word, too, was available for St Paul to use, and it bore a meaning very suitable for his purpose.

'Grace' is the anglicized form of the Latin *gratia*, which was used to translate the Greek *charis;* and *charis*, which was already in common use in classical Greek, occurred also quite frequently in the Greek version of the Old Testament, the Septuagint. In ordinary Greek usage it meant 'gracefulness', 'charm'; 'graciousness', 'favour', 'kindness'; 'a favour', 'a kindness'; and even sometimes 'a (magic) charm'. It could also mean the properly graceful or gracious response of one who has received a kindness, namely 'gratitude' or 'thanks'. In the Septuagint it was used occasionally to translate the Hebrew word *chesed*, which is variously rendered in our English versions as 'mercy', 'lovingkindness', 'steadfast love'; but more commonly it represents *chen*, which is generally translated as 'favour' (and sometimes 'grace'), and which means

---

[1] E.g. in his teaching about forgiveness, and in his making himself a 'friend of publicans and sinners'. See below, pp. 34f. and 106-10.

[2] Especially in the thought of God's 'election' of Israel, which depends on no merit in Israel, but on God's spontaneous, paradoxical love (cf. Deut 7⁷).

characteristically favour shown without obligation, especially by a superior to an inferior.

Now St Paul takes this word *charis*, in the sense of favour freely bestowed, and applies it to God and to Christ. Again and again he speaks of the *charis* of God and the *charis* of our Lord Jesus Christ. What he means by this is hardly anywhere better illustrated than in 2 Corinthians 8[9], where he writes: 'For ye know the grace of our Lord Jesus Christ, that, though he was rich, yet for your sakes he became poor, that ye through his poverty might become rich.' The same idea, though without the word 'grace', is expressed in Philippians 2[5-8], where it is said of Christ that 'being in the form of God' He 'counted it not a prize to be on an equality with God, but emptied himself, taking the form of a servant, ... and being found in fashion as a man, he humbled himself, becoming obedient even unto death, yea, the death of the cross'. Grace, therefore, means incarnation and atonement; it means that act of God in Christ, by which He has shown His favour to us men. And here indeed is favour shown by a superior to an inferior, especially when we recall that it is shown to sinful men, who in no sense deserve such favour, but rather its opposite.

More than once, St Paul sets grace in contrast with sin. 'Where sin abounded,' he says, 'grace did abound more exceedingly' (Rom 5[20]); 'for all have sinned, and fall short of the glory of God; being justified freely by his grace through the redemption that is in Christ Jesus' (Rom 3[23-4]). The same idea finds expression in other words when he says: 'For while we were yet weak, in due season Christ died for the ungodly. ... God commendeth his own love toward us, in that, while we were yet sinners, Christ died for us' (Rom 5[6-8]). The death of Christ on the Cross is thus an act of divine grace on our behalf; it is a divine favour shown to the utterly undeserving and unworthy, a favour motivated by God's own love for us, and by that alone. Grace, therefore, can be described as the love of God in action, entering into the life of humanity to succour and save. It is giving and forgiving love, selfless, self-sacrificing love, powerfully manifested among men and redemptively at work on their behalf.

When the activity of divine love is called grace, what St Paul has particularly in mind is the freedom of it, and that in three respects.

(1) First of all, grace is free in that it is unmerited. It is given freely, not earned. St Paul repeatedly contrasts grace with law and the works of the law, insisting that we are saved by grace, not works (Eph 2^{8-9}). We do not earn our salvation, as workers earn their wages (Rom 4^4); we are justified freely by God's grace (Rom 3^{23}). That was how St Paul had found it in his own experience. 'By the grace of God I am what I am', he says (1 Cor 15^{10}), referring to the experience that had turned him from a persecutor into an apostle. This was something that had not come about through any willing or doing of his own; for indeed, he had not been seeking, but resisting, God and His grace, even while he imagined he was serving God. Nevertheless he had had grace given to him to be a minister of Jesus Christ to the Gentiles (Rom 1^5, Gal 2^9, etc.).

(2) The close and frequent connexion in Pauline thought between grace and the Gentile mission reveals the second main aspect of the freedom of grace—namely, its unrestricted nature, its universality. God's gracious favour, His will to save, is not directed only to Israel, the 'chosen people', but to all mankind. 'For there is no distinction between Jew and Greek; for the same Lord is Lord of all, and . . . Whosoever shall call upon the name of the Lord shall be saved' (Rom 10^{12-13}). God has 'shut up all [men] unto disobedience, that he might have mercy upon all' (Rom 11^{32}), and His redeeming activity in Christ transcends not only the deep division between Jew and Gentile, but all divisions whatsoever of race, class, culture, creed, or sex (Gal 3^{28}, Col 3^{11}), 'for there is no respect of persons with God' (Rom 2^{11}).

(3) But in yet a third sense St Paul insists on the freedom of divine grace. As he wrestles (in Rom 9–11) with the problem of the rejection of Christ by Jewry, and—as we should put it—the

fewness of Jewish converts to the faith, he comes to speak of the 'election' of grace. God in His grace, for His own purposes, has called and chosen only a 'remnant' of Israel (Rom 11[5]). This remnant, it is true, is for St Paul a sign and guarantee that God has not finally and irrevocably cast off His ancient people. Yet it is equally true, that, in the meantime at any rate, 'he hath mercy on whom he will, and whom he will he hardeneth' (Rom 9[18]). Here we have the assertion of the freedom in the sense of the sovereignty of grace. It may be that St Paul's arguments on this subject strike us as both unconvincing and unattractive; but at least they make it clear that we must not think of grace as a mere kindly benevolence that is at everyone's beck and call.

This point is reinforced if we consider the connexion and contrast between grace and certain other terms, such as righteousness and wrath, in Pauline thought. Both Jews and Gentiles are 'under sin', as St Paul sees it, and therefore they are subject to divine wrath (Rom 1[20]–3[20]). The fact that the Jews have the law, as the Gentiles have not, makes no difference; for 'the law worketh wrath' (Rom 4[15]). If the Gentiles are sinners because they have refused to have God in their knowledge (Rom 1[28]), the Jews are sinners because they have a zeal for God that is not according to knowledge (Rom 10[2]). The Jews are in a position like that of Paul himself when, as a Pharisee, he persecuted the Church. He was seeking righteousness, but his own righteousness, on the basis of the law; and this only served to put him more and more in the wrong with God. There is a righteousness of the law, of course, but it is of no avail for salvation (Phil 3[6-7], Rom 9[30]–10[4]). On the basis of the law, men may establish a certain righteousness of their own by doing the works of the law; but this cannot justify them, or set them right with God (Rom 3[19-20]), since it does not alter their basically wrong relationship to God, their essential sinfulness. Hence, over against both Gentile unrighteousness and Jewish law-righteousness, St Paul sets the righteousness of God. This righteousness, which is revealed in the gospel (Rom 1¹⁷) and has been supremely manifested in the Cross of Christ (Rom 3²⁵⁻⁶), is given to men as a free gift (*dōrea*, Rom 5¹²⁻²¹); and as it is received by faith, it can also be called the righteousness of faith (Rom 9³⁰, 10⁶).

Those who receive God's gift of righteousness are 'vessels of mercy'; those who do not are 'vessels of wrath'. But the former have no cause to pride themselves on their position, for it is not due to any merit of theirs, but to God's grace alone (Rom 11¹³⁻²⁵). They must realize, moreover, that the gift of God puts them under obligation to devote themselves wholly to its service (Rom 6¹²⁻²³). They have no licence to sin because they are 'not under law, but under grace' (Rom 6¹⁵). God intends that grace should 'reign through righteousness unto eternal life' (Rom 5²¹); and even if eternal life is not the 'wages' of righteousness, but is God's *charisma* or 'grace-gift', yet it still remains true that 'the wages of sin is death' (Rom 6²³), and that impenitent sinners are storing up wrath for themselves in 'the day of wrath' (Rom 2⁵).

St Paul sees the wrath of God at work in several major directions: (i) in the moral and spiritual corruption of the heathen world, of which he describes the symptoms (Rom 1¹⁸⁻³²); (ii) in the moral and spiritual failure of all but a remnant of Israel (Rom 2, 9); (iii) in the punitive functions of the State as 'a minister of God, an avenger for wrath to him that doeth evil' (Rom 13⁴); (iv) in the universal fact of death (Rom 5). In all these things the wrath of God is 'revealed from heaven against all ungodliness and unrighteousness of men'; and it stands in sharp contrast to the righteousness of God that is revealed in the gospel. But the contrast must not be taken to mean that God is *un*righteous when He visits men with wrath (Rom 3⁵⁻⁶). We must hold that He is righteous, not only when He shows mercy, but no less when He displays His wrath—even though the impenitent sinners who are the objects of His wrath can neither help their sinfulness nor the hardness of their impenitent and unbelieving hearts (Rom 9¹⁴⁻²¹).

The problem of the relation between the righteousness of

wrath and the righteousness of grace, however, is one that St Paul never quite succeeds in clearing up. The best he can do is to argue that the rejection of Israel in no way means that God has failed to fulfil His ancient promises, since these promises were made for those who have faith (Rom 10); and further, that the rejection, which is only temporary and is offset by the fact of the elect remnant, was necessary to the fulfilment of God's purpose for mankind as a whole (Rom 11). It is greatly to his credit that he refuses to turn a blind eye to unpalatable facts, and that he does not seek to resolve the tension between wrath and grace by weakening or denying the reality of either. But he leaves us with the alternative of saying either that there are two kinds of righteousness in God, or that His righteousness as revealed in the gospel is effectively concealed in the revelation of His wrath.[3]

But let us return to the concept of grace, which, as has been said, is essentially the redemptive activity of God in Christ. It must now be noted that this is not simply an activity of the past, but one that continues in the present; and it continues, in particular, through the apostolic preaching of the gospel. This, and all that follows from it, is part of the activity of grace. When St Paul says (with reference to the rest of the apostles) 'I laboured more abundantly than they all' he hastens to add: 'yet not I, but the grace of God which was with me' (1 Cor 15[10]). Elsewhere, speaking of the 'ministry of reconciliation' given to the apostles by God, he says: 'All things are of God, who reconciled us to himself through Christ. . . . We are ambassadors therefore on behalf of Christ, as though God were intreating by us . . .' (2 Cor 5[18-20]). So God in His grace

[3] The latter is certainly the truth. Both wrath and grace are to be thought of as expressions of divine love. Love is the ultimate reality of existence, the final law of life. If we live at cross-purposes with it, lovelessly and selfishly, we find it at cross-purposes with us, and experience it as wrath. If we awaken to our condition and repent, then love meets us as grace; and love's wrath has no other aim but to bring this about. It has nothing in common with the ill-natured reaction of offended self-importance. Still, wrath does conceal love; for although it is an expression of love, it is of a kind to make us think we are hated rather than loved—unless and until it makes us cry out for mercy and so leads us to grace.

continues and extends through the apostles the work accomplished by the incarnation, Cross and resurrection of Christ; and as He does so, grace 'is multiplied through the many' or (as the *RSV* puts it) 'extends to more and more people' (2 Cor 4^{15}).

Now, as a result of the 'multiplication' or extension of grace in this way, we must notice that there are also certain extensions of the meaning of the term. (i) When the gospel is proclaimed, and accepted in faith (as alone it can be accepted), men come to 'stand in grace', to be in a state of grace (Rom 5^2; cf. 1 Pet 5^{12}); that is to say, they enter into a relation to God that is determined solely by His grace. (ii) Grace then becomes a power in men's lives, as St Paul can testify from his own experience. When he prayed for deliverance from the disability of what he calls his 'thorn in the flesh', he received the answer: 'My grace is sufficient for thee: for my power is made perfect in weakness' (2 Cor 12^9), and he found it in fact to be so. (iii) Moreover, grace at work in men's lives produces a similar grace in them. It leads the Macedonians, for instance, to overflow in a wealth of liberality (2 Cor 8^{1-9}). They ask it as a 'grace' (i.e. 'favour') to be allowed to take part in the contribution to the relief fund, which itself is a 'grace' (i.e. 'kindness'; *RSV*, 'gracious work'); and in this St Paul urges the Corinthians also to participate, reminding them of 'the grace of our Lord Jesus Christ', who poured out all His divine riches in order to enrich us men. (iv) Finally, all that we call the graces of the Christian character flow from this grace, as do also the *charismata*, the many and various grace-gifts that are given to individual Christians for the service and building-up of the body of Christ, which is the Church (1 Cor 12^{27-31}, Rom 12^{3-9}, Eph 4^{7-16}).

TWO

Baptism as a Means of Grace

IN THE concluding verses of St Matthew's Gospel, we read that before His Ascension our Lord gave commandment to 'make disciples of all the nations, baptizing them into the name of the Father and of the Son and of the Holy Ghost'. This statement is widely and not unjustifiably questioned, inasmuch as the earliest Christian baptisms were performed, not in the Triune Name, but in the name of the Lord Jesus. Yet even granted that the formula is not original, it would seem unduly sceptical to assert that our risen Lord never gave any commandment to baptize. For the primitive Church from the very first preached and practised baptism in the conviction that such was His will; and the New Testament knows nothing either of unbaptized Christians or of the debates, so widespread today, about the necessity, meaning, and value of baptism.

It is true that St Paul is sometimes quoted as setting no great store by baptism; for he thanks God that he baptized but few of his Corinthian converts, and declares that Christ sent him, not to baptize, but to preach the gospel (1 Cor 1^{13-17}). But here the apostle is dealing, not with the doctrine of baptism, but with a threat to the unity of the Church; and he reminds his readers of their own baptism, not in order to disparage it, but to use it in support of his appeal for unity. So far from depreciating it, he rather protests against the perversion of its meaning by the attachment of undue importance to the person who administers it. After all, he was baptized himself (Acts 9^{18}, 22^{16}), as he assumes the readers of his epistles to have been;[1] and while he may generally have left baptizing to others who had been appointed for it, yet he did on occasion himself baptize (Acts

---

[1] E.g. Romans 6—written to Christians not personally known to him.

19⁴⁻⁷, 1 Cor 1¹⁴⁻¹⁶). Furthermore, he cannot mean to suggest any opposition between preaching and the sacramental rite, since baptism belongs to the gospel, and he himself more than once names it in connexion with the Cross of Christ, which is the very heart of his preaching. In the New Testament, the proclamation of the gospel to those outside concludes with the appeal: 'Repent ye, and be baptized . . .' (Acts 2³⁸); and for the instruction, exhortation, and encouragement of those already baptized, their baptism frequently furnishes the text.

The situation is very different today, when baptism is often a subject for discussion and debate, but all too rarely for preaching. The reason for this is not far to seek. Baptism has become divorced from its original connexion with the gospel, so that questions can be asked about it such as never occurred, and could not occur, to the first Christians.

The gospel is the proclamation of the mighty work wrought by God when He sent Jesus Christ into the world. It is the message of how, through the incarnation, death, and resurrection of His Son, God has inaugurated a new, divine order of life in the midst of the old order of this world. It declares that as He once delivered ancient Israel out of bondage in Egypt and instituted the Old Covenant, so now He has accomplished a far greater deliverance and established a New Covenant and a New Israel through Christ. It asserts that in Jesus Christ, God Himself has entered into our world of sin and death; by His death and resurrection He has decisively broken the power of evil to which the children of Adam are subject; and this He has done out of pure grace in order to furnish a way of redemption for all mankind.

The gospel is the good news that God has given our sin-polluted, death-doomed race a new start and a new hope. By raising up Christ as our Saviour and Lord He has initiated a new creation, he has made a beginning of the resurrection of the dead and the regeneration of the world. For Christ is not simply a figure of past history, existing by and for Himself alone; He is the Second Adam, the head of a new humanity. He is the head over all things to the redeemed humanity of His body, the Church, of which all Christians are members. This body is also the temple of the Holy Spirit (1 Cor 3^{16}, 6^{19}), a habitation of God in the Spirit (Eph 2^{22}), into which all Christians are built as living stones (1 Pet 2^5). But the temple of Christ's body is only in process of construction and growth, and it is by Christ Himself, through the Spirit, that it is being built up. The chief means employed for this building up of the Church are the Word and sacraments of the gospel, whereby Christ calls men to himself, incorporates them into His body, and makes them partakers of the New Covenant and heirs of the Kingdom of God.

Now inasmuch as the Church is the body of Christ and the temple of the Holy Spirit, the preaching of the Word and the administration of the sacraments can be said to be acts of Christ and acts of the Spirit. They are acts performed by Christ Himself through the instrumentality of His body; for just as the movements of my hand or tongue (which are members of my body) in obedience to my will must be attributed to me, so the actions of members of Christ's body in obedience to His will must be attributed to Him. The sacraments are such actions, since they are not instituted and celebrated by our human initiative, but in obedience to the commandment of Christ. In a similar way, the sacraments can be said also to be acts of the Holy Spirit, since it is under the impulsion of the Spirit of Christ that the members of His body act in obedience to their Head; and their actions (in so far as they are obedient) are expressions of His Spirit. For just as the spirit of a man finds expression in what he says and does—that is, in the actions of his tongue and other members of his body—so the Spirit of Christ can find expression in words and acts performed by members of His body. Hence sacramental rites, which consist of words and actions willed and commanded by Christ, give expression to the Spirit of Christ, the Holy Spirit.

To the profane mind, it is true, the sacraments consist merely of human speech and actions—just as the Church consists of merely human institutions and associations of men, and even our Lord Himself is no more than a man, doubtless a most extraordinary man, but still merely a man. But faith, which agrees with the gospel that Christ is the fullness of the Godhead in bodily form, and the Church is the Body of which He is Head, unhesitatingly asserts that the gospel sacraments ordained by Christ are very far from being merely human rituals. For just as the human lips and limbs of Jesus did not make His words and deeds any less divine, so the human administration of the sacraments does not exclude, but manifests, the work of God. That is how the sacraments are able to be what we claim them to be: 'means of grace' and media of Christ's Real Presence among men. The Presence is realized, of course, in the sense of 'made real', through the Holy Spirit; and it is realized in the sense of 'apprehended by us', through faith—though its reality is in no way dependent on our faith, but on the faithfulness of God in Christ.

Enough has now been said to enable us to understand St Paul's saying that 'in (*or* by) one Spirit were we all baptized into one body' (1 Cor 12^{13}), and to see how he can speak of baptism as 'the seal of the Spirit' (Eph 1^{13}, 4^{30}; cf. 2 Cor 1^{22}). By our baptism, which is an expression of the Spirit of Christ, we are stamped, so to speak, as belonging to Christ, and incorporated as members into His body. Alternatively, baptism can be called 'the circumcision of Christ' and described as 'a circumcision not made with hands' (Col 2^{11}). That is to say, baptism is a mark of membership in the New Israel under the lordship of Christ, just as circumcision was a mark of membership in the Old Israel under the leadership of Moses. It is, however, a mark 'not made with hands'; and since this term elsewhere in Scripture (2 Cor 5^{1}, Mk 14^{58}) signifies something of divine, not human, origin or devising, we may take it here as supporting our view of baptism as an act of God and of Christ (cf. Eph 5$^{25-7}$). This view of baptism, incidentally, is no doubt the reason why the New Testament displays so little interest in the precise details of the baptismal rite, or in the person who administers it. Nothing seems to be essential but the use of water and the Word.

In baptism, therefore, it is God with whom we have essentially to do; or rather, God has to do with us. For here in unfathomable grace he condescends to our weakness and sinfulness, and shows Himself Immanuel, God with us. Here God in Christ, through the Spirit, sets His seal upon us, establishes His covenant with us, makes us members of His church, and pledges us a share both in the fellowship of Christ's sufferings and the power of His resurrection.

To be incorporated as members into the Church which is the body of Christ is to belong to a Body so closely united with its Head that its members can be said quite simply to have been baptized 'into Christ'. Membership in Christ's body, therefore, carries with it participation in all that belongs to Christ, and not least in His death and resurrection. For anything that happens to the head of a body is bound to be of significance for the body itself and its members. Hence St Paul can say: 'Are ye ignorant that all we who were baptized into Christ Jesus were baptized into his death?' (Rom 6³). He also says that we have been baptized into a participation in the resurrection; and here he uses a very striking expression, saying that we have been 'planted together' (*symphytoi*) with Christ. 'If we have been planted together with him in the likeness of his death', he asserts, 'we shall be also in the likeness of his resurrection' (Rom 6⁵). That is to say, by our baptism we are engrafted, so to speak, into Christ as branches into the True Vine (Jn 15⁵); we are brought into a vital relation to the Saviour, placed where we can receive His salvation.

The meaning is not essentially different when baptism is described as 'washing of regeneration' (Tit 3⁵); for through baptism we are born into that new order of existence which God has established through Christ. By our natural birth we belong to a race that is under the dominion of sin and death; we are members of the body corporate of sinful humanity (the 'old man'), and our whole existence is subject to its conditions

BAPTISM AS A MEANS OF GRACE

('original sin'). By our baptism we are set in an entirely new context (the 'new man'); we become members of the new humanity whose Head is Christ, and which in Him participates in the life of the new age as heir of the promises of God (cf. Gal 3^{27-9}). This does not mean that any psychological or metaphysical change takes place in us by virtue of our baptism, as is shown by the fact that the same thought can be expressed in quite different terms. What happens in baptism is comparable to the passage of Noah and his family in the Ark from the old world before the Flood to the new world after it (1 Pet 3^{20-1}), or to the crossing of the Red Sea and the deliverance of ancient Israel out of bondage in Egypt (1 Cor 10^2). Baptism is thus the dividing line, as it were, or the point of transition between the old order of existence and the new; and to the new order all those 'regenerated' by baptism properly belong—whether they acknowledge the fact or not.

At the same time, if the new age has dawned, it has not yet been consummated; nor will it be, until Christ is manifested in glory. We therefore who belong to it by virtue of our incorporation into Christ have still to live in the old order of the present evil world. We have died with Christ, yet we still have to die; we have been raised with Him, yet we still have to attain to the resurrection of the dead. If we have been begotten again, it is to a living hope which will be finally fulfilled only 'in the regeneration when the Son of Man shall sit on the throne of his glory' (Mt 19^{28}). Like ancient Israel, we Christians have been redeemed from our house of bondage, but we have still to enter our Promised Land. In other words, that which has been given to us in our baptism has still to be realized; the meaning and promise of our baptism has still to be fulfilled.

Baptism, therefore, is not merely an act of initiation. It has reference to the whole of the Christian life, which consists of an ever-renewed dying with Christ and rising with Him. Christ has died unto sin once for all (Rom 6^{10}), and so we as members of His body must also die to sin. We must die out of that 'body of sin', as St Paul calls it (Rom 6^6), which is the body corporate of sinful humanity to which we belong by nature. For we have been united with Christ in order that, as He was raised from the dead, so we might walk in newness of life (Rom 6⁴). Being participant in His death and resurrection (Col 2¹²), we must no longer accept the standards of the old order and live by them (Col 2²⁰⁻³), but must mortify our members that are on earth (Col 3⁵), and seek the things that are above, where Christ is, seated at the right hand of God (Col 3¹). We must remember that, just as many of His ancient people whom God delivered out of Egypt were lost in the wilderness, so it is perilously possible for members of the new Israel to come to disaster in their journey through the present world (1 Cor 10¹⁻¹³). In such terms as these, the Scripture again and again recalls us to our baptism, warning us not to be fashioned according to this world, but to be transformed by the renewing of our mind, exhorting us to put off the old man and put on the new.

But if baptism thus furnishes the text for warning and exhortation, it no less provides a solid ground for confidence and hope. For just as circumcision was a seal of membership in the Old Covenant that God made with ancient Israel, so baptism is the seal of the New Covenant that God has made with us. It is something not of our doing or devising, for we did not baptize ourselves, but we were baptized; and that is also something that can never be taken away from us. It is therefore a perpetual assurance to us that we belong to God's people. If there are those who tell us that we do not really belong to Christ's church, because we lack some qualification necessary for admission to their denomination or society, we need not be disturbed, for our baptism refutes them. If our conscience accuses us, we need not despair, since God's covenant, sealed to us by baptism, is always in force, and the very essence of it is the forgiveness of sins (Jer 31³⁴, Mt 26²⁸, Acts 2³⁸, 22¹⁶). That is why it is described as a 'washing' and associated with justification and grace (Tit 3⁵⁻⁷, Rom 6⁶⁻⁷; cf. 1 Cor 6¹¹). Hence, even if we fall away and break our connexion with Christ, the Covenant still remains as a ceaseless call to us to return in penitence to the grace of baptism and the life in Christ. It is God's own Covenant, which He Himself has made with us, and nothing but our own rejection of it can deprive us of its blessings.

Since Christian baptism is, as we have seen, an act of Christ and of the Holy Spirit, it possesses a significance that is entirely independent of any willing, doing, or desiring, not to mention deserving, of those who are baptized. It is an act of pure grace, by which we who are wholly undeserving are adopted into the family of God. (For the Church, the body of Christ and the temple of the Holy Spirit, is also called 'the household of God'; Eph 2[19], cf. Gal 6[10].) Now, when a child is adopted into a human family, his adoption signifies two things in particular that are worth noting. First, he is the object of love and care on the part of his adoptive parents, and that is why they adopt him. He is not loved because he is adopted, but he is adopted because he is loved. Secondly, he is unquestionably a member of the family, with all the privileges and responsibilities that that entails. As he grows up, he may or may not respond rightly to those privileges and responsibilities; he may even one day repudiate them. Or if (improbably but conceivably) he were to be abducted, he might lose all possibility of responding to them. But nothing of this in any way affects the reality of his adoption and the place made for him in the family, which is an expression of parental love and care, not of a satisfactory filial response. And the position is precisely similar when God in our baptism adopts us. By our baptism we are made members of the household of God, so that we may grow up as children of God through the grace of our Lord Jesus Christ and the fellowship of the Holy Spirit.

Christian baptism belongs to the gospel and is an expression of the gospel. It is a gift of God's unmerited and unmeritable grace, his prevenient grace. That is why it is right that infants should be brought for baptism; for God's grace is always prevenient. The New Testament, it is true, says nothing explicitly about infant baptism. But the argument from silence is notoriously precarious, and there are good reasons for not making too much of it here. If infants shared in the deliverance of ancient Israel from Egypt, would infants be excluded from the new Israel and the redemption wrought by Christ? If infants eight days old were sealed by circumcision as members of the Old Covenant, would the seal of the New Covenant be refused to any infants there might be in those households that were baptized? (Acts 16^{15}, 1 Cor 1^{16}). Or must we suppose that greater qualifications were required for admission to the covenant of grace than to the covenant of law? The fact is that the Lord who meets and receives us in baptism no more demands certain qualifications of us than He did of those concerning whom he said: 'Suffer the little children to come unto me. . . .' The narrative from which these words come (Mk 10$^{13-16}$) has doubtless been preserved because it served to answer the question, already raised in the primitive Church, whether little children could receive a blessing from the Lord; and it is well that we are reminded of it in the Baptismal Office. Yet even apart from such considerations as these, the baptism of infants would still be entirely legitimate and desirable.

Inasmuch as baptism is fundamentally something that God does, a blessing that God gives through Christ, there is no *essential* difference between the baptism of infants and that of adults and 'believers'. The much-discussed question whether infants can have faith is really irrelevant here—though they might perhaps have as much faith as the daughter of the Syrophoenician or of Jairus, or as the Centurion's servant, all of whom received a blessing from the Lord; and the Church that baptizes them generally has at least a little faith on their behalf. But what is more important is that baptism, like the gospel which it embodies, is not constituted by any man's believing, but is a work of divine grace; and this the baptism of infants makes more abundantly plain. Just as the New Covenant was instituted, so the seal of it is given to us, not by any willing or doing of ours, but by grace alone. The advantages and benefits of it are appropriated, it is true, only by faith, but faith is not their creator; and we are not baptized because we have already appropriated them, but *in order that we may be assured of them and encouraged to believe*. This applies no less to the baptism of older persons than of infants. They are not baptized on the ground of any qualifications they might be thought to possess, and lest we should suppose that they were, the word is spoken to them: 'Except ye turn, and become as little children, ye shall in no wise enter into the kingdom of heaven' (Mt 18^3).

Is baptism, then, necessary to salvation? In one sense we may not say that it is, for God is presumably able to reach men with His saving grace by other means than the gospel sacraments, or even perhaps than the gospel word. But since it is by the Word, or the preaching of salvation through Christ, that He has reached us, we are bound to attend to what He tells us in that Word; and the Word itself speaks of the sacraments and bids us observe them. We might well remember also that our Lord Himself did not disdain to be baptized, so that it ill becomes us as His followers to minimize the value and importance of baptism. Let us suppose that a wealthy well-wisher offered each of us a cheque for £10,000. Would it not (to say the least) be extremely ungracious of any of us to ask whether he could not give us the amount in cash and spare us the trouble of going to the bank? Of course he could, but he would presumably have his reasons for preferring the cheque. And just, so, God has doubtless His reasons for giving us the sacraments. What His reasons are, moreover, we may perhaps in part divine.

The sacraments stand guard against both an over-intellectualization and a false spiritualization of the gospel. They warn us against equating saving faith, on the one hand, with the mere acceptance of a creed, and on the other, with a simply subjective, psychological mood. And they constantly remind us that salvation, the gift of God, is given and received only in and through the Church, the body of Christ. In the sacraments, as in the Incarnation which is the theme of the gospel, 'God comes down, he bows the sky, and shows himself our friend'; and it is a defective faith that refuses to recognize and meet Him there. The deliberate rejection of the sacraments means a failure to take quite seriously the message of salvation through the Word made *flesh*. Hence, although we certainly may not say that an unbaptized person cannot be saved—as if baptism were the only means of grace, or as if it were a kind of passport, without which entry into heaven would be barred—yet we may just as certainly insist that the rite of baptism, like the sacrament of the Lord's Supper, is essential to a full and adequate presentation of the gospel. Individuals and groups (like the Quakers) may manage well enough without it, but it may be questioned whether they would manage so well if the Church as a whole were not maintaining its sacramental witness all around them.

Baptism, therefore, is not a kind of 'optional extra', possibly useful, but in no sense necessary to the divine plan of salvation. Even if it were, it might well be regarded as very desirable, when we recall that not only all the New Testament Christians, but even our Lord Himself, thought it fitting to be baptized. But the value and importance of baptism have come to be questioned, of course, because its essential meaning has been obscured and misunderstood. It has not been recognized in its true nature as an occasion and means of the gracious, personal action of God in Christ, whereby He adopts us into the household of His church and makes us heirs of His salvation.

Not that we should imagine there is anything 'magical' in the sacramental rite. It does not automatically ensure that the baptized will enter into their inheritance. (Nor, we may add, does it mean that the Church can be defined as consisting simply of all baptized persons.) For all too many who have crossed the Red Sea of baptism, whether in infancy or in riper years, perish in the wilderness of unbelief. Too many who (to change the figure) have been engrafted in the True Vine by grace never become rooted in it by faith, and bear no fruit. Too many who have been adopted into the family of God are, so to speak, abducted from it by irresponsible parents and guardians who do not fulfil their promise to give them access to the teaching and worship of the Church. And too often the Church itself takes its own responsibilities in this matter all too lightly. Yet the fact that so many baptisms are fruitless does not render any baptism meaningless; and it is no more of a problem than the fact that the preaching of the gospel, which evokes faith in some, hardens others in their unbelief. Here we must ask with the apostle: 'Shall their want of faith make of none effect the faithfulness of God?' (Rom 3³).

Naturally, it is of importance that the meaning of baptism should be understood, and the Church that practises baptism has a solemn obligation to expound it. For just as preaching that neglects the sacraments is defective, so sacraments that are never preached are bound to be ineffectual. The blessing they convey is appropriated by faith alone, but 'faith cometh of hearing, and hearing by the word of Christ' (Rom 10¹⁷). Hence the Church must do all it can by preaching, teaching, and pastoral care to lead the baptized in the right way. They are like someone who has inherited a vast fortune. If they are infants, this must be administered for their benefit by parents and guardians until they come of an age to claim it for themselves. If they are already of age, they can claim it forthwith; but it can be forfeited by neglect, or squandered by misuse. The baptized, therefore, must be taught the meaning of their baptism, and instructed, encouraged, and exhorted on the basis of it. Because they have been baptized, it is not less but more necessary to work and pray for their conversion, their personal appropriation of what their baptism means, and for their continued growth in grace thereafter.

Christian baptism confers a great privilege and a great responsibility. More steadily than our own feelings or even our faith, it attests both God's unmerited love for us and His unceasing claim upon us. It engrafts us into the True Vine, not because we have borne fruit, but in order that we may; and this we can do only as we abide in the Vine, drawing life from the parent stem—and submitting to the pruning-knife of the Husbandman (Jn 15¹⁻⁸). In other words, baptism makes us members of the Church which is Christ's body, not because we have already found salvation for ourselves, but in order that we may find it in Him. For Christian salvation is no private affair of the solitary soul, but a participation (by faith) in the common life that is imparted by the Holy Spirit through the Word and sacraments of the gospel to the members of the body of Christ. To such participation our baptism continually calls us, bidding us take our place in the fellowship of Christ's church, to which we properly belong. For 'Christ also loved the church, and gave himself up for it; that he might sanctify it, having cleansed it by the washing of water with the word, that he might present the church to himself a glorious church . . . that it should be holy and without blemish (Eph 5^{25-7}).

THREE

Justification as a Work of Grace

IN ITS doctrine of justification the Christian faith possesses a succinct and striking means of expressing its own distinctive character. This is not the only, nor the only legitimate, means which it possesses, but it may reasonably be claimed as the most suggestive and challenging. Yet the doctrine of justification, at least under that name, can hardly be said to hold a prominent place in modern Christian discussion and propaganda. The very word 'justification' (which is used freely enough in ordinary speech) seems to strike a jarring note in a religious context. Associated pre-eminently with two, or perhaps three, great names in Christian history, it seems to belong, with them, to the past. But it is surely not without significance that these names have become symbols of epoch-making moments in Christendom, moments when the gospel, threatened with eclipse or largely obscured, suddenly shone forth again in full vigour and undimmed.

The Apostle Paul, Martin Luther, and John Wesley, despite all distance of time and dissimilarity of circumstance between them, have one thing in common. Each of them wrestled with the same personal problem; each of them found the same answer; and each proclaimed his discovery, with startling and well-known results. Their problem was the fundamental religious question, how they were to adjust their relationship to God; their answer was the specifically Christian solution, formulated in terms of the doctrine of justification. Whatever else may have influenced the men and their work, this problem and its solution furnished the dominant impulse of their lives. Their one supreme aim was to present the gospel to their world in all its fullness and unalloyed.

It is not, however, the intention of this chapter to discuss the historical emergence and development of the doctrine of justification, nor to enter into the controversies that have been raised around the outstanding figures we have named. Its intention is rather to show how the Christian doctrine of justification provides an effective, if summary, formulation of the essence of the Christian gospel; how it answers in a way that cannot be surpassed the fundamental question of all religion; and how it adequately meets the deepest needs of human life.

The word 'justification' itself is a term with legal associations, and its theological usage is coloured by the legalistic conception of religion typical of Judaism.[1] God is there conceived as the righteous Judge, who will one day judge every man in strict accordance with His law. The law is the expression of God's holy and righteous will, and in the Judgement only those who have conformed to its requirements will be 'justified' or pronounced righteous. No one who has transgressed the law of God has any hope of justification, unless he repents; that is, unless he ceases from disobedience and learns to obey; for God 'will not justify the wicked' (Ex 23[7]). According to the verdict finally pronounced, reward or punishment will be meted out. The righteous will 'enter the kingdom of heaven', and 'inherit eternal life'; the wicked and sinners will be excluded from the kingdom and forfeit the life. And since in the present world it is generally the wicked who prosper and flourish, while the righteous suffer and are despised, the final reckoning will mean a vindication of righteousness to which the godly can look forward with eager longing and hope.

From this Jewish view the Christian differs profoundly, though its terminology is very similar. God is still a righteous Judge, and the awe of His judgement remains. It is still only the justified who gain the life of the kingdom of God. The law is still an expression of God's will, and as such is 'holy and just and good' (Rom 7[12]). Indeed, the deepest intention of the law is

---

[1] By Judaism here is meant, not the faith of the Old Testament, but that post-exilic development of the religion of Israel which found its most characteristic expression in Pharisaism.

JUSTIFICATION AS A WORK OF GRACE

first truly seen when it is interpreted and fulfilled by Christ, who sums up the will of God for us in the words: 'Ye therefore shall be perfect, as your heavenly Father is perfect' (Mt 5^{48}). This, however, is to demand the impossible. Even the most scrupulous observance of the law does not attain this; and in the light of Christ it is only too plain that 'all have sinned, and fall short of the glory of God' (Rom 3^{23}). (Or will anyone seriously claim to be as good as Christ, as good as God? Yet God wills nothing less.) Who, then, can possibly be justified?

It is at this point that the astonishing and revolutionary thing happens. God, who abominates the unjust human judge (Prov 17^{15}, Ex 23^7), actually 'justifies the ungodly' (Rom 4^5); he opens the kingdom of heaven and grants eternal life to sinners. And this He does on the ground of His pure mercy and grace alone, out of His freely given and unmerited love. The sole condition required on man's part is faith: what is offered must be accepted, the gift must be received, the grace appropriated.

The term 'justification' has often been criticized as too redolent of the law-court for Christian use, where it is said to introduce an improper and even dangerous note into theology. There is an element of truth in this criticism, especially if we consider only the etymology of the word. Etymology, however, is rarely a safe guide to doctrine, for the real meaning of any word is only to be found in its context; and from the context we have just outlined it should be clear that even in Judaism 'justification' is not something purely forensic. It is never a mere verdict of acquittal and nothing more, but it is an acquittal that carries with it admission to God's kingdom and a share in His eternal life. A similar caveat should, incidentally, be entered regarding other terms which may be used to express the same idea as justification. The remission or forgiveness of sins, for instance, never means the mere cancellation of a debt.

However that may be, when Christianity speaks of 'justification by faith' or 'by grace', or 'the justification of the sinner', it is clear that if we are in a law-court, a remarkable change has taken place in the atmosphere. In fact, the language of the law-court has been used, with deliberate intent, to destroy the very idea of legalism in religion. Free forgiveness is neither the rule nor the exception in a court of law; still less a forgiveness of this kind, which means not simply that the case is dismissed, but that the guilty sinner is received into fellowship with the holy God.

Now if, in the broad outline we have drawn, we have rightly interpreted the Christian meaning of justification, it is not difficult to see that it does effectively formulate the essential content of the gospel. Thus far we have considered it simply in idea, but we may now turn to the reality which underlies this idea. On what grounds does Christianity base its paradoxical view? If Judaism expects the justification of the righteous at some Great Assize in the future, where and how is the justification of the sinner realized according to Christianity? The answer to these questions lies in the content of the Christian message; that is, in Jesus Christ. In the Incarnation, Cross and resurrection of Jesus Christ, and in His church with its Word and sacraments, the idea of justification finds its concrete reality; these are the facts on which the theory is based.

When the Christian faith affirms that in Jesus Christ the eternal and living God is present among men, this can only mean that God does in fact receive sinners into fellowship with Himself. The teaching of Jesus itself is sufficient to dismiss all thought of human merit or desert as a factor determining God's dealings with men. God makes His sun shine and His rain fall on the just and the unjust, and is kind to the unthankful and the evil (Mt 5^{45}, Lk 6^{35}). The wages of the Labourers in the Vineyard bear no relation whatever to the hours they have worked (Mt 20^{8-16}). The Publican, who appears before God as a sinner with nothing to plead, goes home 'justified', rather than the scrupulously dutiful Pharisee who claims his reward (Lk 18^{9-14}). Such a claim is absurd, for even when men have done all that is commanded, they can say no more than 'we have done that which it was our duty to do' (Lk 17^{10}). Who can claim a reward for meeting his obligations?

But what is already clear in the teaching of Jesus becomes even more plain from His conception and fulfilment of His own mission. 'I came', he says, 'not to call the righteous, but sinners' (Mk 2^{17}); and He became notorious as one who 'receiveth sinners, and eateth with them' (Lk 15^2). He came 'to seek and to save that which was lost' (Lk 19^{10}), and He created a scandal by becoming 'a friend of publicans and sinners' (Mt 11^{19}). There were even occasions when he plainly and explicitly anticipated the prerogative of God, and pronounced to sinners the absolution and remission of their sins (Mk 2^5, Lk 7^{48}).

Here, however, a problem arises which might well have been raised above, and which certainly occurred to those who observed the behaviour of Jesus or heard the preaching of Paul. If Jesus deliberately cultivates the friendship of publicans and sinners, must He not be a sinner Himself? If God 'justifies the ungodly', how can He be righteous Himself? The answer is that He can and He does—at the cost of the Cross. This answer is indicated, though not elaborated, where St Paul speaks of Christ as one 'whom God set forth to be a propitiation, through faith, by his blood, to shew his righteousness . . . that he might himself be just, and the justifier of him that hath faith in Jesus' (Rom 3^{25-6}).

It is of course beyond our province here to examine all that is involved in the 'propitiation', or to examine the many and varied theories of the Atonement. What is of importance is that when the holy God enters into fellowship with sinful men, He can only do so at this great price. As a matter of historical fact there were only two possible ways in which Jesus could have avoided the Cross: He could have acquiesced in human sin, or He could have left sinners to their fate. He could have accepted the standards of value and the understanding of life maintained by the men whose fellowship He sought, or else He could have withdrawn Himself from their society. But in neither case would He have fulfilled His mission; and He therefore refused to do either, though He knew that the refusal must inevitably lead to the Cross. He offered men His fellowship, but on His terms and not theirs; and the friendship of the Son of God for sinful men quite literally cost Him His life. It is little wonder, then, that the Cross has become the supreme sign and seal of divine grace and love, since 'while we were yet sinners, Christ died for us' (Rom 5[8]).

Were it not for the Incarnation and the Cross, the idea of justification would be a mere theory, if it had ever existed at all. But were it not for the Church with the Word and sacraments of the gospel, the Incarnation and the Cross would scarcely be more than an ancient tale. It is through the fellowship of the Church, the body of Christ, animated by His Spirit, that justification becomes a present reality for all who believe. The Church is the medium through which He still continues His characteristic work of love. When the Word of the gospel is preached, it is Christ Himself who, through halting human words, still comes 'to call sinners'. When the Bread is broken and the Wine poured out, it is Christ Himself who still 'receiveth sinners' and shares with them His very life. Whenever 'two or three' are met in His name, He is there present with His own (Mt 18[20]). It is here that 'justification' is realized, for it is here that He leads sinful men into real and actual communion with the living, holy God.

The essential meaning of the Incarnation, the Cross and the Church is crystallized in the doctrine of justification; and this meaning is the ground for saying that the doctrine answers, in a way not to be surpassed, the fundamental question of all religion.

All real religion is, or claims to mediate, communion with the eternal, fellowship with God. The question of questions for any religion, therefore, is how this fellowship or communion is brought about. The difference between the various religions is nowhere more apparent than in the different answers they give to this question when it is put to them. Broadly speaking, however, there are only two main types into which they can be divided. Either the realization of fellowship with God depends

JUSTIFICATION AS A WORK OF GRACE

primarily on something that man does or is, or else it depends primarily on what God is and does. In Judaism we have seen an example of the former type. Man finds favour and acceptance with God if he fulfils the law; for then he is righteous, and can rightly claim a place in God's kingdom; that is the due reward of his merit. In Christianity we find precisely the opposite. Man finds favour and acceptance with God, simply because God wills to show favour to him; in himself he is a sinner, who has no claim to a place in God's kingdom; and if he receives a place, it is by the free gift of God's grace and unmerited love. Beyond the point which Christianity thus reaches, it is impossible to go; for here the realization of man's fellowship with God is conditioned solely, and not just primarily, by God.

It is true, of course, that even in Christianity there is a condition to be fulfilled on man's part if he is really to enter into fellowship with God; he must have faith. It must be a faith, moreover, that acknowledges God as 'the justifier of the ungodly', the forgiver of sins. That is to say, faith in the Christian sense of the word is inseparable from repentance, or the confession that one is a sinner and the willingness to be forgiven. For the offer of forgiveness, or justification, as it is proclaimed in the gospel, implies the judgement that those to whom it is made are in fact sinners. To offer forgiveness is not to pretend that no wrong has been done, but to assert that it has. That is no doubt why many people do not like the gospel, for they are unwilling to believe that they are sinners. On the other hand, there are those who are only too painfully conscious of their own sinfulness, but are unable to believe in God's willingness to forgive them. Consequently, although 'all have sinned' and Christ 'died for all' (2 Cor 5[14]), so that God's grace and love are freely offered to all, yet not all men live in fellowship with God, not all have faith.

Does not this, then, suggest that in the last resort we must say that even in Christianity the realization of fellowship with God depends at the decisive point on man? Or shall we say that faith itself is the gift of God, and so risk becoming entangled in the problems of predestination? With those problems we cannot deal here, though something will be said about them in a later chapter; but at this point two observations may be made. First, if faith is a 'condition' of fellowship with God, it is one quite unlike that constituted by the 'works' of legalistic religion. These meritorious deeds profess to form the legitimate basis of a claim to divine favour; but faith is not the basis of any claim. It is rather the actual claiming and appropriating of a favour that is freely offered. In Judaism the favour is absent if the works are lacking; but in the gospel the favour is there whether faith is present or not. To say that justification is 'by faith alone' is to describe the human aspect, so to speak, of a relationship which in its divine aspect exists 'by grace alone'. Both phrases sound the death-knell of all legalism and merit.

Secondly, when faith is asserted to be a gift of God, this is in order to prevent its ever being regarded as another kind of 'work' or meritorious achievement on the part of man. The gospel does not say 'Unless you have faith, God will not love you', but rather 'God loves you, therefore have faith, believe in His love for you'. Faith, in the Christian understanding of it, is a human response to the forgiving love of God. That is why we cannot lightly disregard the assertion that faith itself is a gift of God. Such faith would be a literal impossibility apart from the divine grace of the Incarnation and the Cross and the unceasing initiative of divine love through the Church. We could not be justified and enter into fellowship with God through faith if He did not draw from us that response by the revelation of His grace.

The reality of this divine love, that humbles itself and takes the form of a servant for the sake of an utterly undeserving world, is what vindicates the claim of Christianity to be the final and absolute religion. That does not mean that there are no traces of divine initiative in other religions, for without action on the part of God there could be no religion at all. But in no other religion is the divine initiative so central, so sovereign, so complete. For whenever God becomes a factor of serious moment in a man's life, so that the question of his relationship to God grows urgent, it seems to be a natural assumption that man must in some way become worthy of God and attain to God's level in order to have communion with Him. Whether by his own efforts or with divine aid, man must scale the heights in his quest for God. Christianity, however, puts an end to all this; for it both effects what all religions seek to do, and at the same time rejects their methods. So far from being yet another form of man's age-long quest for God, it proclaims God's own quest for man; and it offers a real and certain communion with God, not on the high level of God's holiness, but on the low level of man's sinfulness. There can be no certainty or assurance of attainment, where everything depends on what man achieves; but here the emphasis is placed, not on man, but on God and His unfathomable grace. And it is on God that the emphasis ought to be placed in any religion worthy of the name. If God is really to be God, He must be sovereign and supreme; and He is never more truly God than the exercise of His justifying grace.

At this point, however, an obvious objection can be raised. When Christianity offers fellowship with God 'on the level of sin' (Nygren), it undoubtedly meets the deepest religious needs of man, but it might well seem to do so at the expense of destroying the foundations of his ethical life. If God receives the sinner so freely, is there not every reason for making the antinomian assumption that ethical considerations are irrelevant? If heaven is not gained, nor hell avoided, by seeking to do what is good and right, why should we trouble to do it? Why should we not 'continue in sin, that grace may abound?' (Rom 6^1).

The shortest answer to this question is St Paul's 'God forbid!'; but it is not difficult to see that more can be said than this. To begin with, it should be clear that if we seek to do what is good and right as a means to some end beyond itself, we are not really doing what is ethically good. To practise honesty because honesty is the best policy is not really to be an honest person at all, and to obey the commandments of God from fear of hell or hope of heaven is not really to do the will of God. It is rather to do our own will, since our eye is on the end that *we* wish to attain—namely, our own salvation. From this difficulty, however, the doctrine of justification delivers us. The justified man is set free from any concern about rewards and punishments, and the will of God can be done freely and for its own sake. It is true, of course, that in the New Testament and in the teaching of our Lord Himself there are statements about rewards and punishments in connexion with a Judgement yet to come; and such statements must be taken seriously. But they clearly must not be understood in such a way as to conflict with the principles of our Lord's teaching which we have already observed. How they are to be understood, the following considerations will show.

Just as Judaism looked forward to a final Judgement of the world, so also does Jesus. He therefore distinguishes between present and final justification. In the present time He is the mediator of God's forgiveness to sinners who recognize their sinfulness and need of forgiveness; and this is present justification. But those thus justified and set right with God are more than once warned of the Judgement they still have to face. In this final reckoning, moreover, it seems that the verdict will be pronounced on men according to what they have done or failed to do—that is, according to their 'works'. But it is important to notice the nature of these 'works'. For Christians, the disciples of Jesus, the question will be whether they have openly confessed their faith in Him (Mt 10^{32-3}) and have been obedient to the will of His Father (Mt 7 $^{21-3}$), persisting in faith to the very end (Mk 13^{13}) and showing to others a forgiving and merciful spirit like that which has been shown to them (Mt 18^{23-35}, 6^{14-16}, 5^7). In other words, the 'works' by which they are to be judged are nothing else but the evidence of a living faith.

The question is not dissimilar with regard to the heathen, whose Judgement is described in the parable of the Sheep and the Goats. Naturally nothing is said here about faith, or the confession of Christ, but instead the verdict is pronounced according to certain 'works' that men have or have not done.

JUSTIFICATION AS A WORK OF GRACE

But again it is important to notice the nature of the works. They are nothing else but works of mercy, acts performed simply and solely for the purpose of helping those in need. This fact is emphasized by the surprised questions of the parties concerned, both on the right hand and the left (Mt 25$^{37, \ 44}$). Neither group is conscious of having performed (or omitted to perform) acts by which they would be judged in the sight of God. But their unselfconscious behaviour, motivated by no thought of its possible future consequences in the shape of reward or punishment, reveals the kind of persons they are, and whether they are the kind who belong to God's kingdom or not. Jesus is always more concerned about the kind of people we are than about the legal rectitude of our conduct, as He shows supremely by His interpretation of the law in the Sermon on the Mount. And the right kind of people are for Him those who are merciful as the heavenly Father is merciful, who is kind to the unthankful and the evil (Lk 6$^{35-6}$).

The relationship between present justification and future Judgement, as Jesus conceives it, can be very well illustrated from the parable of the Unmerciful Servant (Mt 18$^{23-35}$). Here is a man who has contracted an immense debt, which he cannot possibly pay, and he thoroughly deserves to be punished. But when he pleads for mercy, and for time to pay, even greater mercy is shown to him than he requests; for his debt is quite simply cancelled. This is an act of pure grace on the part of his master. Yet immediately afterwards the man shows that he has completely failed to appreciate its significance, by refusing to show any mercy to a fellow-servant who owes him a quite trifling debt. He shows himself, that is to say, entirely out of tune with his master; and he forfeits the kindness that has been shown to him, because he has never really grasped it. Not that he would have earned or merited it, even if he had shown mercy to his fellow-servant, for we do not have a *right* to the forgiveness of our debts because we forgive our debtors.

If, therefore, we are justified at the Last Judgement, this is as much an act of grace as our present justification. There is nothing meritorious in the 'works' to which reference is made in connexion with it. In the case of Christians, such works are nothing else but evidence of living faith—that is, of a right response to the grace that has been shown to them in Christ. In the case of the heathen, the works are evidence that they are the kind of people to whom the gospel of grace would have appealed, and who will find themselves entirely at home in the kingdom of a gracious God.[1] The absence of such works, in the case of anyone who has had opportunity to perform them, is quite clear testimony that the person concerned has nothing in common with God and His kingdom, and would be quite out of his element in heaven. For what place can there be, for one who does not believe in showing mercy and forgiveness, in a kingdom where mercy and forgiveness are the supreme characteristics of the King?

In the light of what has now been said, a final point may be added with regard to the relation between justification and sanctification. It is sometimes said that in present justification God accepts the sinner with a view to, and in anticipation of, his sanctification, which is something that he cannot attain without divine aid, but which is the necessary condition of his final justification. It is not, however, difficult to see that in this view we have a rationalization of the doctrine of justification, which is little else but a very thinly disguised legalism. Undoubtedly it is true that God wills our sanctification; He does not want us to remain sinful, but to become holy and righteous and good; and that is something which is possible for us only through communion with Him. But we may not therefore say that God justifies us, or takes us into fellowship with Himself, simply in order to make us good. Fellowship with God is not a means to an end, but an end in itself. Religion is not the handmaid of morality, although in modern preaching it is often represented as such.

---

[1] The heathen who are saved, though they never had the opportunity to respond to the gospel, may perhaps be thought to have responded to the 'grace of Creation', of which something is said in a later chapter.

JUSTIFICATION AS A WORK OF GRACE

Justification and sanctification must certainly never be separated, but they can and must be distinguished. Sanctification is neither the purpose nor the cause of justification, but rather its result. It is the fruit of faith, the effect of grace. Not that entire sanctification is the immediate result of present justification. The sinner who is received into fellowship with God is still a sinner, and he is likely to remain a sinner to the end of his earthly days. He has acquired, without doubt, a new motive and centre for his life, but the old centre does not disappear forthwith. He is not yet wholly God-centred, but is still in some measure self-centred, so that we might describe him as, in the literal sense of the word, 'eccentric'. He is *simul justus et peccator*, both righteous and a sinner; and although he becomes daily more sanctified as his communion with God deepens and grows, there is no promise that the final goal will be reached in the present world.

At the same time, it must be emphasized that the Christian doctrine of justification nowhere suggests that God accepts the sinner in easy-going tolerance of his sin, but always in spite of it. The very word 'justification' here proves its value, by reminding us that God is, after all, the Judge, who judges us to be sinners, and whose good and perfect will remains as an absolute obligation for us, even though He justifies sinners. It is in the light of this will that we are seen to be sinners at all—that is, precisely in the light of God's good will toward us. The God who justifies the sinner is the God who makes His sun shine and His rain fall on the just and the unjust, who loves His enemies and gives His only Son to die for them. This selfless, self-giving love is what judges us precisely in the act of justifying us; for *we* do not behave like that. This is the righteousness of God, supremely revealed on the Cross, which both exposes and pardons our sin. And it is such a love as this, which God Himself has given to us, that He desires us to pass on to others. The ethics of justification can be summed up in the words: 'Freely ye have received; freely give' (Mt 10[8]).

FOUR

The Holy Spirit of Grace

IN THE Epistle to the Hebrews, the Holy Spirit is called 'the Spirit of grace' (10^{29}). This expression occurs nowhere else in the New Testament,[1] but its use is apt, inasmuch as it is through the Holy Spirit that the grace of our Lord Jesus Christ is mediated to men; and indeed, the Spirit's mediating work is itself an act of grace, since it means the entry of the Holy into the hearts and lives of sinful men. In this chapter, therefore, we shall attempt to see what precisely is meant by the Holy Spirit, and how His operation is to be understood. In doing so, we shall anticipate a part of our conclusions from the outset by using personal pronouns with reference to the Spirit; for His activity is undoubtedly of a personal nature, however much room for debate there may be as to whether He is 'a person'.

In both Scripture and Creed, the Holy Spirit is represented as the Lord and Giver of life. He is the living and life-giving presence, power, energy, activity of God in the world and the lives of men. Indeed, He is God Himself, for God *is* Spirit (Jn 4^{24}). By contrast, man—like other animate creatures—is described as 'flesh'. When 'spirit' is ascribed to man, as it sometimes is in Scripture, the term is used either as a 'higher synonym' (Wheeler Robinson) for 'soul', emphasizing its origin from God, or else it denotes some special endowment or operation of the divine Spirit in man. The term 'flesh' (or sometimes 'flesh and blood'), however, describes human nature in its totality, body and soul. It refers primarily, of course, to the physical aspect; but it includes also the psychical—just as both aspects are included when we use an expression like 'Don't tell any*body!*' or 'I won't tell a *soul!*'

---

[1] It occurs in the Old Testament in Zechariah 12^{10}.

As contrasted with Spirit, flesh signifies essentially the creatureliness, dependence, frailty, perishableness of man (Gen 6^3, Isa 31^3, 1 Pet 1^{24}). Man has not life in and from himself, but lives only as he receives life from the life-giving Spirit of God (Job 33^4, 34$^{14-15}$; cf. Ps 104$^{29-30}$). This is true, not only of eternal, but also of temporal life, and not only of intellectual and moral, but also of corporeal life. Man has no life at all that is not the gift of God.

The contrast between flesh and Spirit is one of the fundamental contrasts of biblical thought, and sometimes it appears as a sharp opposition. Of this opposition we shall have more to say in a moment, but here it must be stressed that there is no essential or necessary antagonism between flesh and Spirit. The two are not mutually exclusive; the Spirit can dwell in and work through the flesh. The fundamental biblical opposition is not between flesh and Spirit, creature and Creator, but between the Creator of the flesh and its destroyer, between God and the devil, Christ and Satan, the Holy Spirit and the Unholy. These are mutually exclusive, and between them there is a conflict upon whose outcome depends the final destiny, the salvation or perdition of man.

In the biblical view, man, whose nature is flesh, is a creature of God, and as such 'very good' (Gen 1^{31}, 1 Tim 4^4). But in 'the present evil world' he is open to the influence of evil, corrupting powers, to which he has fallen victim, and by which he is estranged from his Maker, alienated from the source of his life, and brought under subjection to sin and death. When, how, or why this originally happened, we do not know. That lies outside the realm of our experience, since we are born as members of a humanity already in subjection. We can therefore speak of it only in mythological terms like those of the story of the Fall of Adam. This may not give us a scientifically or historically tenable explanation of how our present plight originated, but it undoubtedly gives a truthful and revealing picture of *what our plight is*.

Man, who quite literally owes all that he has and is to God, and can live and realize his destiny as man only in complete and unceasing dependence on God, is nevertheless led by an evil, ungodly spirit (symbolized in the story by the serpent) to disavow his indebtedness. Instead of grateful trust and loving obedience toward God, he displays a spirit of self-will, of self-assertion, self-seeking, and would-be self-sufficiency, which both puts him in the wrong with God and corrupts his relationships, not only with his fellow-men, but with the rest of God's creatures as well. Such a spirit, of which we have daily evidence in the newspapers and (if we know how to read it) in our own heart, is certainly not divine. But neither can it be regarded as in any true sense human, for it is destructive of humanity. It is rightly called the devil and Satan, or 'the spirit that now worketh in the sons of disobedience' (Eph 2^2).

It should be noted, however, that man yields himself to this unholy spirit voluntarily. He is not driven and coerced by it against his will, but it operates rather in and through his will. He is therefore not simply an unfortunate to be pitied, but a sinner who in a very real sense deserves his fate. Now it is in this sense—as fallen and sinful—that human nature, or the flesh, can be set in sharpest opposition to the Holy Spirit of God. To see them thus opposed is particularly characteristic of St Paul. But it cannot be too strongly stressed that they are not opposed as two incompatible 'substances', but as the Holy and the unhallowed, or perhaps rather, the Sacred and the desecrated. Hence we must never take their opposition to mean that human nature, either in its physical or its psychical aspect, is intrinsically unholy or evil. If it were, there could never have been an Incarnation: the Word could not have 'become flesh' (Jn 1^{14}), the Son of God could not have taken a 'body of flesh' (Col 1^{22}), and man could not have been redeemed.

We must rather say, then, that there is *in* fallen human nature an unholy spirit which is not *of* human nature, and which can be cast out and replaced by the Holy Spirit. When that happens, the corruption of the flesh is healed, and man becomes what in the purpose of God he is meant to be—truly and fully human.

To the end that it might happen, the eternal Son of God himself became Man in Christ.

Thus far no mention has been made of the fact that the expression '*Holy* Spirit' is characteristic of the New Testament rather than the Old, or—what is much more important—that in the New Testament the Spirit is inseparably connected with Christ and is called the Spirit of Christ. This does not mean, of course, that the Spirit in the New Testament is a different Spirit from the Spirit of God, or of the Lord, in the Old; for the New Testament itself furnishes ample evidence to the contrary. It makes no difference to the meaning, whether the Spirit is described as 'holy' or as 'of God', since holiness is the characteristic quality both of God himself and of everything that belongs to God. The preference of the New Testament for the former description reflects the late Jewish reverential tendency (observable already in inter-testamental literature) to avoid direct mention of the divine Name. Hence it is not in their terminology that the difference between the Old and the New Testament conceptions of the Spirit must be sought. The difference lies rather in the fact that in the New Testament the divine plan of salvation, God's work for the redemption of mankind, has entered on a new phase.

In Christ, God has given our race a new beginning, a Second Adam. By His Incarnation, Cross and resurrection, the age-long conflict between man's Creator and the Adversary of both man and his Creator has been brought to a decisive issue and the opening of its final phase. The new order of the Kingdom of God, the 'age to come' foreshadowed in the Old Testament, has been inaugurated and is moving on to its consummation, the manifestation of Christ in glory. And with this new, eschatological event, there comes, quite naturally, a new, eschatological activity of the Spirit. Some aspects of this we shall consider presently, but there is one point that must be particularly stressed here: the close connexion, and sometimes the virtual identification, which we find in the New Testament, of the Spirit with the risen Christ, living and active in His body, the

Church. This fact securely establishes the nature and significance of the new, eschatological phase of the activity of the Holy Spirit.

This does not mean that the Spirit is now doing something of a totally different kind from what he ever did before—as if, for example, He had abandoned His part in the work of creation for that of redemption. He is the Spirit of the one God who is both Creator and Redeemer both before and after the advent of Christ. We may therefore still regard Him as the giver of our earthly, temporal life, and of every vestige of wisdom, virtue and excellence that is to be found among men in this world. But when we speak of Him as the *Holy* Spirit and the Spirit of Christ, we shall think essentially of His part in the work of redemption from the events of the Incarnation and Pentecost onward. And the close association, which is sometimes a virtual identification, of the Holy Spirit with the living Christ, which we find in the New Testament, is supremely important here. It determines for us the character of the Spirit, giving us a criterion by which to 'prove the spirits, whether they are of God' (1 Jn 4[1]); for no 'spiritual' phenomenon that is out of harmony with the character of Christ, can be attributed to the Holy Spirit. It reminds us, moreover, that no human wisdom, virtue, and excellence, even though it is the gift of the Spirit of God, can escape from the corruption that is in the world through sin, unless the Holy Spirit completes His work by casting out ungodliness and 'the spirit that now worketh in the sons of disobedience' (Eph 2[2]).

Before we go on to look more closely at the redemptive work of the Holy Spirit, it is important to point out that when the Bible and the Christian faith speak of spirits, whether holy or unholy, they are speaking of quite concrete realities of human experience. This fact is often obscured for us by the mythological notions associated with unholy spirits—'demons', the 'devil'—and by the metaphysical problems connected with the doctrine of the Holy Spirit and the Trinity. In the light of modern scientific knowledge, for instance, we naturally boggle at the primitive Christian view of mental and physical disorders as due to 'demon-possession'; and on ethical and theological grounds we find great difficulties in the thought of the existence, and still more of the 'personality' of the devil. Yet, whether or not we are right in rejecting such ideas, we shall be quite wrong if we assume that the 'possession' of human beings by 'unclean spirits' is impossible, or if we shut our eyes to the reality of diabolical forces at work in the world. And we shall land ourselves in even graver difficulties with regard to the Christian estimate of man. We shall be in danger of attributing to human nature itself, evil which is essentially alien to it and destructive of it.

Whether demons and the devil 'exist' or not, there are undoubtedly spiritual forces that are real enough in this world, and human nature is by no means insulated against them. There are ideas, doctrines, ideologies, philosophies of life, in which 'spirits', good, bad, and indifferent, find expression, and through which they influence men. What such spirits may be ontologically, is perhaps an unanswerable question, and in any case we are not concerned with it here; for we have no need to deny their reality merely because we cannot solve the ultimate problem of their nature and origin. Presumably no one would dispute that when we use phrases like 'the spirit of Nazism', 'the spirit of Communism', and many more, we are speaking of quite real factors and forces in human life. Nor can it be denied that what we have described as 'the spirit of self-will, self-assertion, self-seeking, and would-be self-sufficiency' manifests itself in innumerable disastrous ways, in individuals and groups of men and in the human race as a whole. Equally it must be admitted that the Holy Spirit, the Spirit of Christ, is a reality.

Something of the way in which spirits, holy and unholy, operate, may perhaps be illustrated as follows. In the Epistle to the Galatians St Paul asks his readers: 'Received ye the Spirit by the works of the law, or by the hearing of faith?' (Gal 3[2]). The answer he expects is plain: it is 'By the hearing of faith'. Elsewhere he tells us that 'belief cometh of hearing, and hearing by the word of Christ' (Rom 10^{17}). It is thus by hearing and believing the gospel, the message of Christ, that the Holy Spirit is received. Now something very similar to this can be said with regard to other spirits and the way they are received. How, for instance, does a man become imbued with (say) the spirit of Marxism? One answer is certainly: by hearing or reading Marxist propaganda *and believing it*. A person who does not believe it, is unmoved (unless to hostility) by the spirit that finds expression in such propaganda. But the believer receives the spirit. In and through the doctrine which he accepts, the spirit quite literally enters into him; and the more firmly and deeply he believes, the more he becomes possessed of the spirit—that is, he both possesses it and is possessed by it.

Now the more a spirit takes possession of a man, the more it controls him. His thoughts, feelings, speech, and actions are governed by it. Not that it acts coercively, in such a way as to obliterate his personal, individual characteristics, or to move him against his will. On the contrary, it operates precisely in and through these. It works in such a way that (for example) no matter what language or dialect a Marxist speaks, his speech is recognizably Marxian, has a Marxian flavour. This flavour, moreover, is in no way dependent on a sprinkling of quotations from Marx. The spirit is not in that sense bound up with the 'word' or doctrine, although it is conveyed, so to speak, by the 'word'. Instead, it enables its possessor to expound, develop, apply, draw out the implications of Marxian doctrine for changing times and circumstances. Now cannot something similar to this be said with regard to the Holy Spirit? Is not this the way in which our Lord's promise is fulfilled, that 'the Spirit of truth . . . shall take of mine, and shall declare it unto you' (Jn 16$^{13-14}$), and that 'the Holy Spirit shall teach you . . . what ye ought to say' (Lk 12^{12})?

Three further points may be usefully noticed in connexion with the mode of operation of the Spirit.

First, such spiritual forces as we have in mind are 'transcendent', 'supra-individual'. They can take possession, not only of individuals, but of groups and whole communities; and then they can operate, not merely through conscious, intellectual acceptance of the doctrine on the part of individuals, but also in other, often subtler ways. They can find expression in customs, conventions, rituals, laws, institutions, and so forth. They become as it were an atmosphere in which people live and move and have their being; they are 'in the air', as we say. So the spirit of Communism is abroad in many lands, and so the Holy Spirit is in the universal Church.

Secondly, it is only the possession of the spirit of Communism that makes a man a Communist, and only the possession of the Spirit of Christ that makes a man a Christian. One not imbued with the spirit of Communism might very well conform in his conversation and his behaviour to the requirements of a Communist State in which he lived, if only for fear of the consequences of not doing so; but he could hardly be regarded as a true Communist. Similarly, a man cannot be regarded as a true Christian simply because he professes the Christian creed, and seeks to conform his life outwardly to Christian standards. These things can be done, even sincerely and without conscious hypocrisy, in a spirit that is quite other than the Spirit of Christ. But, 'If any man hath not the Spirit of Christ, he is none of his' (Rom 8[9]).

Thirdly, it rarely if ever happens that either an individual or a community is wholly possessed by one spirit alone. Certainly, in the world as a whole, there are many conflicting spirits. There are spirits religious, irreligious, and anti-religious; and the different religions embody different spirits. Even within the Christian Church and in ourselves, as we know from experience, the Spirit of Christ and the 'spirit of the world' are often in conflict. And while the rich diversity of thought and life within the Church can be attributed to the Holy Spirit, it is undoubtedly to the influence of unholy spirits that we must trace the divisions between the 'churches'.

But now, how can we tell whether we possess the Spirit of Christ? What are the effects of His presence and work in human life? We obviously cannot enter here into a discussion of all the phenomena associated with the Spirit in the New Testament, but two main features must be mentioned.

First, the Spirit of Christ is the Spirit of sonship, who 'beareth witness with our spirit, that we are children of God' (Rom 8[16], Gal 4[5-7]). In a certain sense, of course, it is true that all men are children of God—as His creatures, whom He loves as a Father. But fallen and sinful men are no true sons of their Father; their whole attitude to Him and to one another manifests a different spirit from His. They are out of harmony with Him, at cross-purposes with Him. Therefore also He is at cross-purposes with them; His will stands opposed to theirs; they are under His 'wrath'. That is why they must be 'born again' (Jn 3[3-7]) and receive 'the adoption of sons' (Gal 4[5-6], Rom 8[15]), which is the work of the Spirit of Christ the only-begotten Son. Then, as Christ did, they can turn with child-like confidence to God, crying: 'Abba, Father!' (Gal 4[6]).

Secondly, where the Holy Spirit is present, there is love. Love is the chief 'fruit of the Spirit' (Gal 5[22]), through whom God's own love is 'shed abroad in our hearts' (Rom 5[5]). It is a love like that with which Christ has loved us, and has commanded us to love one another (Jn 13[34]). The Holy Spirit is the Spirit of pure, unselfish, self-sacrificing love. That is why it can be said that 'where the Spirit of the Lord is, there is liberty' (2 Cor 3[17]). There is liberty because, being 'led by the Spirit of God' (Rom 8[14]), we are delivered from that spirit of self-will and self-seeking which—however refined and 'spiritual' it can be—prevents us from ever loving and serving either God or our neighbour freely. The Holy Spirit is the Spirit of sonship and brotherhood, whose working in men's lives puts them in a right relation to God and one another.

In the light of these facts it is possible to answer the question about the 'personality' of the Spirit, or at least to see the direction in which the answer must lie. As the Spirit of sonship and brotherhood, He is the fount and source of all truly personal and truly humane relationships, and stands in marked contrast to all unholy spirits, which invariably dehumanize and depersonalize human existence in so far as ever they control it. This is the strongest reason for insisting that the Holy Spirit's own nature is personal, and that He ought to be spoken of in essentially personal terms, no matter how difficult the problem of His ontological status may be.

But let us look again at the work of the Spirit. We have said that He liberates man from the spirit of self-will; but it ought here to be emphasized that this liberation is not accomplished in a moment. Wherever the Holy Spirit gains an entry into human life, there begins that conflict between the Spirit and the 'flesh' (or human nature as sinful and corrupt), of which St Paul speaks in Galatians (5^{17-24}), and that 'wrestling' which, he says, 'is not against flesh and blood, but against ... the spiritual hosts of wickedness' (Eph 6^{12}). If through the Cross and resurrection of Christ, as we stated earlier, the decisive blow has been struck at the powers of evil, the conflict is by no means yet ended, and the final battle has yet to be fought. The work of the Spirit is the continuation of this conflict, which cannot cease until the last vestiges of evil have been cast out of humanity and, indeed, of the whole creation of God. Those who receive the Spirit, therefore, inevitably find themselves caught up into the struggle, engaged against the evil that is in themselves and in the world around.

The means by which the Spirit gains entry into human life is, as has already been indicated, the gospel of Christ, the Word of God. By this Word, spoken through the prophets, incarnate in the Son, proclaimed by the apostles, set forth in Christian preaching, teaching, and sacraments from the beginning until now, the Holy Spirit calls, gathers, and sanctifies men as members of that redeemed humanity which is the Body of Christ, the Church of which He is the Head. It follows, therefore, that the Church—the *visible* Church, in all its variety of denominational manifestations—is the centre of the Spirit's activity in the world. Not, of course, that everyone who is a member of the visible Church is *ipso facto* filled with the Holy Spirit; for the

Spirit is received only by faith—though not necessarily, let it be said, only by *conscious* faith, and certainly not only by conscious orthodoxy. This being so, we may not set a limit for the activity of the Spirit, confining it within the bounds of the visible Church (and least of all may we claim a monopoly of the Spirit for our own denomination). The work of the Spirit is not only directed *to* the Church, but also *through* the Church to the world at large; and He may well also have ways of influencing men other than through the Church. But be that as it may, of one thing we can be certain: wherever the Word and sacraments of the gospel are found, there is the Church and there is the Holy Spirit; and wherever the gospel is accepted by faith (which is the only way it can be accepted), the Spirit enters in and with it into the heart and life of the believer according to the measure of his faith.

The work of the Spirit in the hearts and lives of men, however, is but the 'firstfruits' (Rom 8^{23}) and 'foretaste' (Heb 6^{4-5}) of that which is to be. Not until the Spirit has completely taken possession of our 'flesh' shall we fully realize the destiny for which we have been created; and that is something which is not finally accomplished in 'this world', but only at the consummation of 'the world to come'. But to receive the gift of the Spirit is to receive already a share in 'the life of the world to come', and this is also an 'earnest' (Eph 1^{13-14}), a pledge and guarantee, of that which is to be. As St Paul says: 'If the Spirit of him that raised up Jesus from the dead dwelleth in you, he that raised up Christ Jesus from the dead shall quicken also your mortal bodies through his Spirit that dwelleth in you' (Rom 8^{11}). The end is not until the resurrection of the dead, and that, too, is the work of the Holy Spirit of grace.

FIVE

Dogma as an Affirmation of Grace

I THE PROBLEM OF DOGMA

A GENERATION or two ago, under the influence of liberal theology, it became a common habit to contrast 'the Jesus of history' with 'the Christ of faith'. The teaching of Jesus, or the religion of Jesus, was set in opposition to the doctrines of the Church, and it was assumed that the former represented genuine Christianity, which the Church with its dogmas and creeds had sadly obscured. This habit has by no means entirely disappeared, in spite of the marked change in theological climate that has now taken place, and there are still many who think that Christianity might be far more easily commended to the modern world, if it were divested of 'the trappings and accretions of the ages' and restored to the presumed simplicity of its original, undogmatic form.

Even quite recently it has been argued,[1] that the dogmas of the Incarnation and the Trinity represent a quite disastrous perversion of the original message of Jesus and the apostles. Not that the argument in this case is based on the 'liberal' conception of the Jesus of history, but rather on the reaction from it that is associated with the name of Albert Schweitzer and the doctrine of 'thorough-going eschatology'. The outlook of Jesus and the Primitive Church is supposed to have been dominated, in the manner of late Jewish Apocalyptic, by an expectation of the imminent 'end of the world', which, of course, very soon proved mistaken. Consequently, the original message of Jesus and the apostles must be 'de-eschatologized' in order to make it intelligible and acceptable to modern man. It had, in fact, to be de-eschatologized already in the Early Church; but there the problem was tackled in the wrong way, and the development of

[1] In *The Formation of Christian Dogma*, by Martin Werner.

dogma was the result, which we are now called upon to repudiate.

It must, however, be said at once that no solution of the problem of dogma can be found by seeking to be rid of dogma altogether. There never has been, and never can be, an 'undogmatic Christianity', and to attempt to produce one is to show a singular lack of understanding both of the true significance of dogma and of the nature of the original Christian faith; for the primary document of Christianity, the New Testament itself, is dogmatic from beginning to end, as it is not difficult to show. No further evidence is required than the constant recurrence of the formula 'Jesus Christ'. These two words point, it is true, to a historical figure, a man of the first century AD; but they point to Him as something more than that—namely, as an object of religious faith. The Jesus of history, whether we conceive Him in terms of the 'liberal' or the 'eschatological' or any other interpretation, is not and never could be, as a purely historical figure, the object of faith. He might be a prophet, a teacher, or a 'religious genius' and the founder of a religion; but it is not as such that the New Testament primarily represents Him.

Of all the New Testament writings, the Synoptic Gospels no less than St Paul or the Fourth Gospel, it could be said with equal truth: 'These are written that ye may believe that Jesus is the Christ, the Son of God; and that believing ye may have life in his name' (Jn 20[31]). The writers are by no means uninterested in the Jesus of history, but they are not interested in Him as biographers or historians; their purpose is rather to bear witness to their own faith in Him as the Christ, and to evoke and establish a like faith. Hence the very first Christianity that ever existed, was neither 'the teaching of Jesus' nor 'the religion of Jesus', but 'faith in Jesus Christ'. And with this title 'Christ', and the confession of faith in Him, we are no longer in the realm of mere history, but of dogma. It was, moreover, on the basis of this and other rudimentary dogmatic formulae of the New Testament that later dogmatic construction was carried out. Therefore it is plain that we cannot regard dogma simply as a later accretion to Christianity, of which we might as well be rid.

With this fact in mind, the suggestion has often been made that the creeds and dogmas of the Church should be restated in modern terms, clearly intelligible and devoid of offence to the modern mind. We must recognize, it is rightly said, that there is a real problem underlying the slighting references we sometimes hear to 'outworn creeds' and 'antiquated dogmas'. We must recognize that a form of words which in its own time and place was vividly meaningful may cease to convey its original meaning, or even any meaning at all, in a different time and place. This is what has happened to a large extent in the case of the Church's creeds, which nowadays often mean little or nothing to those who have neither inclination nor opportunity for historical research. Hence the plea is put forward, with considerable justification, for a restatement of the faith.

Such an attempt, however, to make Christianity more acceptable to our age involves no slight risk. Restatement can easily come to mean modernization, and modern terms can become a cloak for modern ideas that have little or nothing to do with genuine Christianity. The currently fashionable form of such restatement, launched by Professor Rudolf Bultmann, and known as 'de-mythologizing', furnishes an example of this danger. For while it undoubtedly seeks to preserve (in terms of an Existentialist philosophy) the religious values of what it very questionably calls 'myth', it often seems to do much less than justice to the historical realities with which these values are associated in the New Testament and traditional Christian belief. It tends to dissociate the Christ of faith from the Jesus of history, very much as the Modernists used to do, except that its interest is centred in the former, whereas theirs was in the latter. The demythologizers have certainly understood the concern of the New Testament writers to evoke and establish faith, but they frequently seem to have a very inadequate appreciation of the object of that faith. For while the object of Christian faith can never be a merely historical figure, yet neither can it be simply an idea expressed in a 'mythical' tale, no matter how religiously—or existentially—valuable it may be.

There are, it is true, mythological elements in Christianity, of which the story of the Fall of Adam and the visionary descriptions of the Consummation of the Ages (the 'End of the World') are obvious examples. But it cannot be too strongly emphasized that these depend for their Christian meaning and validity entirely on the central, historical reality of Jesus Christ. The Christian faith does not insist on the 'fallenness' and universal sinfulness of mankind simply on the basis of the story of Adam, but rather, in the light of the knowledge of the glory of God revealed in Jesus Christ, it sees that 'all have sinned, and fall short of the glory of God' (Rom 13[23]), and therefore finds the story of Adam meaningful and relevant. Nor is the Christian hope of man's final deliverance from evil inspired by the dreams or speculations of apocalyptic writers, though the latter can be adapted and used to express a conviction that is grounded on the victory actually won over sin and death through the Cross and resurrection of Jesus Christ. Thus even the 'myths' in Christianity are not mere myths; they have something of the nature of dogma about them. Mythological conceptions are not the source of dogmatic teaching, though they can be employed as a vehicle for its expression.

But be that as it may, it is clear that if we are to have any success in commending the Christian faith to the modern world, we must speak the language of our time and place as far as we can. Before we attempt to do so, however, it is above all important that we should know precisely what it is we ought to say in that language; and this is what we are concerned to discover in the present chapter with regard to the traditional dogmatic and credal formulations of the faith. We may, of course, find that some of the things we ought to say are difficult, if not impossible, to translate adequately into contemporary idiom. It is impossible, for instance, to reduce the gospel to terms entirely acceptable to the logical positivist or empiricist; his vocabulary is not yet large enough. But the main thing is that,

DOGMA AS AN AFFIRMATION OF GRACE

before we seek to restate our dogmas in another idiom, we should clearly grasp the meaning that is contained in their own. In what follows, therefore, we shall consider, first, what may be called the formal character of dogma; secondly, its essential content; and thirdly, the problem of its validity.

II THE FORMAL CHARACTER OF DOGMA

We may begin by recalling what was said above about the dogmatic character of the New Testament, with its constant repetition of the formula 'Jesus Christ'. If it is true, as we suggested, that the title of 'Christ' and (we may add) all the other titles applied to Jesus in the New Testament are primitive dogmatic forms, what do these titles mean? When Jesus was called Messiah, the Son, Son of God, Son of Man, the Logos, the Lord, what did these titles signify to those who wrote them, and what can they possibly have to say to the modern man? The answer, in brief, is this. All these designations of Jesus point to one and the same thing; they all indicate a single conviction, which all primitive Christians, and indeed all Christians since, share in common. It is the conviction that in and through the man, Jesus of Nazareth, the Eternal has broken in upon us, the living God has revealed Himself to us. This conviction is expressed in a multitude of different ways: God has made Jesus to be both Lord and Christ (Acts 2^{36}), the Word has become flesh (Jn 1^{14}), God has spoken to us in His Son (Heb 1^2) we have seen the glory of God in the face of Jesus Christ (2 Cor 4^6), and so forth. But no matter how different the forms may be, the content is one and the same: in and through 'Jesus Christ' men have been brought into vital touch with God.

The Christian faith is faith in God and in God alone; that is why no merely historical figure could ever be the object of faith. But the Christian faith is faith in no other God than the One who reveals Himself to us in and through the man Jesus Christ. Jesus Christ is therefore the proper object of Christian faith; and it is this faith that is the content of the New Testament and of all Christian teaching and preaching from the very beginning.

This is also just as definitely the faith that is expressed in the dogmatic formulations of the Early Church, and that can be summarized in the one word 'incarnation'. In the Apostles' Creed it appears as belief in 'Jesus Christ, his only Son, our Lord, who was born . . . suffered . . . was crucified, dead and buried . . . rose . . . ascended . . .'. In the Nicene Creed Jesus is 'very God of very God, begotten, not made, being of one substance with the Father; . . . who for us men, and for our salvation, came down from heaven, and was incarnate . . . and was made man . . .'. In the Chalcedonian Definition this last statement concerning the humanity of Christ is filled out, and he is said to be not only 'truly God' and 'of one substance with the Father as regards his Godhead', but also 'truly man' and 'of one substance with us as regards his manhood'; and the completeness of His humanity is strongly stressed.

Now the Nicene and Chalcedonian formulae, it is true, show an increasing departure from the simply scriptural language of the Apostles' Creed, and the Chalcedonian Definition in particular has been severely criticized on this ground in modern times. It has been said, in fact, to reveal the bankruptcy of Greek patristic theology, which was reduced to employing the wholly unsuitable categories of Hellenistic metaphysics in an attempt to explain the mystery of the Person of Christ. Yet although it uses metaphysical terminology, and is deliberately devised to exclude certain misleading metaphysical speculations—Arian, Apollinarian, Nestorian, Eutychian—it is not itself an essay in speculative metaphysics. It is, as can easily be seen if we are not misled by its superficial appearance, a declaration of faith that stands in the same tradition as the New Testament formulae which we have already noticed.

When the New Testament declares that in and through the man, Jesus of Nazareth, the living God has come to men and taken them into fellowship with Himself, this is expressed in such terms as 'the Word became flesh', or 'God was in Christ'.

But such assertions raise serious difficulties for some types of mind, both ancient and modern. Starting with a certain preconceived idea of divinity, they find it impossible that the divine should so degrade itself as to come into contact with 'flesh', let alone that it should 'become flesh'. The very suggestion seems to them absurd and, indeed, blasphemous. Consequently they try to explain that God did not really become incarnate, really suffer on the Cross, and really die. The divine may have inspired the man, Jesus, but it was not born, did not suffer and die in Him. Or else they argue that the physical nature of Christ was only a phantasm, so that the Son of God merely appeared to be born and suffer and die. Or, again, others would insist that although Jesus Christ was certainly more than a mere man, yet it was not the supreme Deity, the very highest God, who came to us in Him. He could not, for He is immutable, impassible, infinite; so that to speak of His incarnation, which involves limitation, suffering, and change, is a contradiction in terms.

To all such arguments the faith expressed in the creeds replies, that in and through Jesus Christ, God Himself—the only and the supreme God—has come to us, spoken to us, drawn us into fellowship with Himself. We are certain of this, because we are certain that there cannot be any higher Deity, if indeed there can be any other Deity at all, than the one with whom we have to do in Christ (cf. 1 Cor 8[5-6]). Therefore we cannot agree that Christ was merely an inspired man, or indeed anything less than God Himself incarnate; for in that case our fellowship would not be 'with the Father, and with his Son, Jesus Christ' (1 Jn 1[3]), but with some inferior being. Unless we can say that Jesus Christ is 'very God of very God, of one substance with the Father', then our experience of communion with God as Christian believers must be regarded as illusory. And equally, if we refuse to say that He is 'truly man, of one substance with us as regards his manhood', we make our experience illusory. He must be both truly and completely man, or else our salvation, our communion with God, is either illusory or only partial. He 'came to seek and to save that which was lost' (Lk 19[10]), and what was 'lost' was the whole man, body and soul—that is the reason for the insistence on the completeness of our Lord's humanity, with the oddly sounding comment that He was 'of a reasonable soul and body'.

The terms in which all this is expressed may well not appeal to us, and we may feel them to be unnecessarily obscure and inadequate; but it is not difficult to see that in them the Church has sought to give expression to the salvation it has experienced. The Christian experience is that in and through Jesus Christ, God Himself has come to men. But if Jesus Christ is not truly God, then it is not *God* who has come to us in Him; and if He is not truly man, then He has not come all the way to *us men*.

Enough has now been said to make it reasonably clear what the formal significance of dogma is. Its function is to give expression to religious experience, or the experience of faith. Religious experience, which means the actual realization of fellowship with God in personal life, is naturally something that is not directly communicable. Yet it can be communicated; and the most immediate, the least indirect, communication possible is by way of what we call 'dogma'. Dogma is the religious interpretation or elaboration of an experienced historical fact or event. The modes of expression may vary at different times and in different circumstances, yet in so far as they are truly dogmatic, they will be religious expressions of religious experience. This point must be stressed. They are religious expressions as distinct, for instance, from scientific hypotheses or philosophical theories or poetic interpretations. Dogma is essentially expression, declaration, proclamation; it is a kind of preaching, a form of the Word of God. As such it is entirely distinct from all attempts at explanation on either scientific or speculative lines. If the Creeds of the Church had been intended as explanatory, for instance, of the Person of Christ, we should be obliged to confess that they are singularly unsuccessful.

No doubt the human mind will always be inclined to try to explain how such things as our dogmas affirm could be possible.

DOGMA AS AN AFFIRMATION OF GRACE 63

We shall always have Christological theories, doctrines of the Person of Christ, offered in explanation of the Incarnation. But such doctrines can never be more than precarious metaphysical speculations; for if we could really explain how 'the Word became flesh', we should have to be the Word ourselves. *How* it happened is wholly outside the realm of our experience; *that* it happened is not, and the fact that it happened is what the dogma declares. Speculative, theoretical explanations of the dogma are not, of course, necessarily useless. They attempt to state, in terms of the thought of the day, such a case for belief that the modern man will find it less difficult to accept. They can have, that is to say, a considerable apologetic value. On the other hand, there is always a grave risk that these metaphysical interests may obscure the main significance of the dogmas they are intended to serve. They can all too easily divert attention from the fundamental religious import, from the gospel which it is the primary function of dogma to proclaim. Dogma, let it be said again, is a religious expression of religious experience; it is a declaration of faith and nothing else.

III THE ESSENTIAL CONTENT OF DOGMA

But let us now look a little more closely at the content of our Christian dogmas, and ask what is the nature of the faith they declare or the gospel they proclaim. More than a hint of the answer to this question has already been given in the preceding discussion, where we have stated that the dogma of the Incarnation is an affirmation that in and through Jesus Christ the living God Himself has come to us men; but in what follows we shall consider along with the dogma of the Incarnation two other dogmas which can also claim to be quite fundamental to the Christian faith—namely, those of Creation and Resurrection. In these three dogmas we have affirmations in the first place concerning God, and secondly concerning ourselves and the world we live in. They affirm in the most concrete manner that God is a living God, actively and effectively at work in the world; that He is sovereign over all existence and all events; and that His sovereignty and activity are the sovereignty and activity of grace. They also affirm by implication that the world is utterly dependent on the divine will; that evil is essentially alien to it as the good creation of God; and that by the sovereign grace of God it is going to be delivered from evil.

We have not space here to take up all these points, but we must at least look at the most central and fundamental of them, which is that God is in His essential nature pure grace. This is plainly the burden of the dogma of the Incarnation. In the Christian view, man is separated from God, not simply nor primarily as creature from the Creator, but as sinner from the Holy One. The fellowship of man the creature with God his Creator is not only possible, but purposed. Empirical man, however, as a sinful creature, is not in such a relation to God as he should be, and he is incapable of bringing about the conditions necessary for it; left to himself he is 'lost'. The Christian faith offers no theoretical explanation of how this state of affairs has come about, either in the Bible or the Creeds; but it does offer an answer to our human predicament, in the shape of a practical solution of the problem, when it proclaims the gospel of the Incarnation.

In the situation where man is alienated from God, and unable to find any way to Him, God himself has made a way for Himself to man. In Jesus Christ He has 'for us men, and for our salvation' come 'down from heaven'; He has come 'not to call the righteous, but sinners' (Mk 2^{17}); He has offended many by being 'a friend of publicans and sinners' (Mt 11^{19}), and by eating and drinking with such people. That is the way of God's dealings with lost humanity. And if many are offended by such ungodly behaviour, and conspire to crucify Him, there are also many who, as they see how 'the Son of Man came not to be ministered unto, but to minister, and to give his life a ransom for many' (Mk 10^{45}), can only assent to the apostle's word: 'God is love' (1 Jn $4^{8, 16}$). That is the nature of God; God in His very 'essence' is pure, spontaneous, unmotivated love. This is the nature of that 'substance' in which, according

DOGMA AS AN AFFIRMATION OF GRACE

to the Creed, Christ is one with the Father; this is the 'fulness of the Godhead' which we see 'in bodily form' (Col 2^9) in Christ; it is 'the glory of God in the face of Jesus Christ' (2 Cor 4^6), who is 'the image of the invisible God' (Col 1^{15}).

The full depth of divine grace and love is seen only in Jesus Christ, but the dogmas of Creation and Resurrection are also dogmas of grace. Before we attempt to show how this is so, however, it should perhaps be emphasized that these dogmas, like that of the Incarnation, are not and do not claim to be anything else but dogmas. When we affirm in the Creed: 'I believe in one God . . . Maker of heaven and earth, and of all things visible and invisible', we are not (for instance) asserting our belief in the literal accuracy of the first chapter of Genesis. We are not asserting anything at all about the way in which God proceeds with His creative work. The dogma of Creation has nothing to tell us about *how* God is Creator; it simply asserts *that* He is. In other words, it neither is nor is meant to be an explanation of the origins of existence, on the lines of scientific or philosophical theory, but is rather an affirmation about the nature of God and His relation to the world and ourselves.

Something similar is true also with regard to the dogma of Resurrection. This does not furnish us with any description of *how* the dead are raised, or 'with what manner of body they come' (1 Cor 15^{35}). It simply asserts as a matter of fact *that* God is one who raises the dead. Very varied views have been held as to when and how the resurrection should take place—just as various views have been held regarding the mode of creation and incarnation—and such views have not seldom been mutually inconsistent. With these, however, we are not concerned here. Our purpose is rather to understand the meaning and content of our dogmas dogmatically—that is, precisely in their character as dogmas, or affirmations of faith in God.

At this point, however, in view of the definition of dogma given above, the question may well be raised whether the dogmas of Creation and Resurrection are true dogmas. For of what 'experienced historical fact or event' can either of them be said to be an 'interpretation or elaboration'? Must it not be admitted that they have no historical reference, and that they ought therefore to be regarded as mythological, if not quite simply mythical?

In answer to these questions, it must of course be admitted that both of the dogmas in question have mythical associations. They have connexions with non-biblical and pagan myths, of which faint traces can still be seen in the biblical accounts of them. Yet they are not simply myths. For not only in Christianity, but already in ancient Israel, they have an essentially historical basis. It was as a result of the historical experience of the Exodus, with the religious significance which this continued to have throughout their subsequent history, that the Israelites came to believe in both Creation and Resurrection. They knew God first as their redeemer and deliverer, who had drawn them into covenant-fellowship with Himself, making a people out of those who were no people, and giving a future to those who had no future. They then came to recognize in the creator of their national existence the Creator of the world, and in the maker of their future the One who both could and would restore life even to the dead.

In a similar way, the Christian belief in God as Creator and Restorer of life is bound up with a further and still more decisive historical event, namely the life, death and resurrection of Jesus Christ.[2] Through him, Christians know themselves to have been brought into a new covenant-relation to God, whereby they have been given new life and hope; and in this they see a work of boundless divine love and grace, which they cannot but confess to be sovereign over all existence and over death itself.

[2] The resurrection of Christ is as historical an event as his crucifixion, if it ever took place at all; for it is both dated and located in close proximity to the crucifixion, and there is evidence for it of the same historical kind. We find it easier to accept the historicity of the crucifixion, no doubt, because crucifixions have been fairly common in history, and we know how they are carried out, whereas the resurrection is a unique event, and we cannot produce anything like it ourselves. But the uniqueness of the event is no justification for a denial of its occurrence, though it might possibly justify the description of it as 'supra-historical' (which some prefer), so long as this is understood to include and not exclude its essential historicity.

DOGMA AS AN AFFIRMATION OF GRACE

Whatever mythical associations the dogmas of Creation and Resurrection may have, therefore, they cannot be regarded simply as myths. They may find expression at times in more or less mythological terms—the account of creation in Genesis 2 is an example of the more, and that in Genesis 1 of the less—but essentially they are rather to be regarded as dogmatic affirmations of things after which true myths have groped.

But let us return to the point that the dogmas of Creation and Resurrection are themselves dogmas of grace. This means that each of them in its own way bears testimony to the same divine love that is first seen in its fullness in Christ. How this is so in the case of Creation, we may perhaps allow St Augustine to suggest. In one of his sermons he argues that before we were created we neither deserved nor desired anything, either good or bad (we could not, for we did not exist), and therefore 'it is grace by which we have been created'. He then goes on to point out that after we were created we sinned, and therefore neither deserved nor could expect anything but evil and damnation, so that it is a still greater grace by which we have been redeemed through Christ.[3] In other words, it is in Christ alone that we see the whole length and breadth and depth and height of divine love; but the Creator is the same God as the Redeemer, and His nature and His name are also love. For in Christ we find, not a new God, other than the Creator and Lord of whom the Old Testament speaks, but a new 'covenant' from God, a new knowledge of God and communion with God, provided by the same divine mercy and grace to which we all owe our existence. It is by divine love that we and all things have been created 'out of nothing'—for whatever else that phrase may be thought to mean, it certainly emphasizes that creation is the free and generous bestowal of gifts on recipients whose ability to receive them is itself a gift. It is, moreover, by the Creator's love (as our Lord points out) that the sun continues to shine and the rain to fall on those who have proved themselves quite unworthy of His gifts (Mt 5[44-5]).

[3] *Serm.* XXVI. xii.12.

Precisely the same divine love and grace is reflected also in the dogma of Resurrection. When we declare our belief in 'the resurrection of the body' (or of 'the dead' or 'the flesh', as at various times it has been expressed), we are simply affirming our faith in God as one who in His sovereign grace restores even the dead to life. And this is indeed grace, since there is clearly nothing the dead can do to motivate or merit the divine gift of new life. The idea of resurrection implies that if the dead are not also—in colloquial phrase—'done for', that is due solely to the omnipotence of divine grace. No doubt it is more attractive to regard death in the Greek way, as the liberation of some unquenchable 'divine spark' or 'immortal soul', which is the essential man, from the prison or tomb of the mortal body. Then the dead can be more optimistically considered as having obtained release from an unhappy bondage and entered into a life more worthy of the name. But that is not the Christian view, either in the Bible or the Creeds. There the body cannot be regarded with contempt, since it is one of the good creatures of God and in no sense a temporarily necessary evil from which we must long to escape. Nor can death be regarded as a friendly liberator, but rather as the 'last enemy' of man (1 Cor 15^{26}), and an enemy that only God can conquer. Man has not life in himself, but is dependent for his existence both here and hereafter on the sovereign activity of divine love and grace; for the God of grace alone has immortality (1 Tim 4^{16}).[4]

[4] Although in the Christian view human personality by the will of God survives bodily death, mere survival is not immortality. There can be survival in hell, which is a living death; but immortality means participation in the life of God and His kingdom. It is attained by entering into communion with God through Christ, who has 'abolished death, and brought life and immortality to light through the gospel' (2 Tim 1^{10}) and has thus made it possible even for us men to become 'partakers of the divine nature' (2 Pet 1^4). To do this means to live by and in that divine love which 'never faileth' (1 Cor 13^8), having it 'shed abroad in our hearts' (Rom 5^5) and knowing that not even death can separate us from it (Rom 8^{38-9}). It is from this that the Christian hope of immortality springs, and the assurance that our perishable, mortal nature will in the end 'put on immortality' (1 Cor 15 $^{53-4}$); though even then we shall not be immortal in our own right, but only as eternally abiding in the kingdom of God.

IV THE VALIDITY OF DOGMA

We must look finally at the question of the validity of dogma, and here it will be relevant to consider, first of all, the history of the word 'dogma' itself. It is, of course, a term of Greek origin, and it was originally employed in political and civic life to signify a public decree or edict. In time it was adopted for philosophical purposes, and came to mean a fundamental principle or axiom. In virtually this sense it was taken over by the Christian Fathers, and since the days of the Apologists it has been used to indicate such ideas as are held by the Church to express essential truths of divine revelation. Not unnaturally, the original sense of the term, as public decree or authoritative edict, continued to exert some influence, and ecclesiastical dogma acquired, or claimed, an authority akin to that of law. This was particularly the case, of course, with regard to the credal statements and definitions promulgated by the great Councils of the Church. Two ideas are thus fused in the conception of dogma: that of fundamental principle or axiom, and that of authority or binding law.

Now if the claim to be authoritative is characteristic of dogma, there are grounds for that claim which at least merit attention. These are partly of an intrinsic, partly of an external nature. Dogma claims authority by reason of the fundamental religious reality which it represents; its authority lies in its own intrinsic worth. But it also claims the support of the universal testimony of the Church; and herein lies its external authority. As an expression of divine truth, attested by the common witness of the Church, dogma claims the right to be heard and received. It is true, no doubt, that the intrinsic worth of dogma is precisely what its critics call in question; but they might surely be expected to pause before pitting their own personal judgement against the massive testimony of the ancient and general consent of the Church. Unfortunately, the external authority of dogma, which is the authority of the Church, is no less exposed to attack than the claims based on its intrinsic worth. For the authority of the Church is not essentially different in nature from that which dogma claims in virtue of its own inherent quality. Church and dogma, in fact, stand together, since the Church itself is a dogmatic conception.

In the Christian understanding of it, the Church is not merely an empirical society or institution, a historical phenomenon, but is itself a dogma. As a human society, its history can be traced in a manifold variety of forms from apostolic times to the present day. But it cannot be historically demonstrated that this society is, as Christians claim it to be, the 'elect race' and 'holy nation' of the People of God, or the New Israel and the Body of Christ. That is something which cannot be proved, but only believed; it is a dogma. It involves a 'religious interpretation or elaboration of a historical fact or event'. That is why the Church rightly has a place in the Creed. Not that the Church here is intended as an object of faith alongside of, or in any way rivalling, our faith in God. The Christian faith is faith in God, and in God alone; and if it can be expressed as faith in the Church, that is only because and in so far as the Church is understood to be an object and instrument of divine activity, a creation of divine grace; for the dogma of the Church, like the other dogmas we have discussed, is also a dogma of grace.

To believe in the Church is to believe that in and through the human, historical institution or society, the God of grace is Himself at work, creating, sustaining and directing it. It is on the measure and intensity of this belief, moreover, that the idea of the authority of the Church basically depends. For unbelievers the Church naturally possesses no authority; for believers it possesses authority in varying measure, according to their differing conceptions (or misconceptions) of the relation between its divine and human aspects, or of the way in which divine grace operates with sinful men. Decisive authority is found by some only in the New Testament Church, by others in the 'undivided Church' of the early centuries, while others find it in their own denomination at the present day; some

DOGMA AS AN AFFIRMATION OF GRACE

attach it to official pronouncements of duly constituted ecclesiastical authorities, while others see it only in the general consensus of Christian opinion; and some regard it as infallible, while others repudiate the very idea of infallibility. In this situation it is clear that the authority of the Church is a very disputable criterion for the validity of any dogma.

Nevertheless, it is a matter of history that the term 'dogma', in harmony with its original political associations, early came to mean something we are commanded to believe on the authority of the Church. It became possible, moreover, for the Church to issue new dogmatic decrees, asserting the necessity of articles of belief that were unknown to earlier generations of Christians. Outstanding modern examples of this are, of course, the Roman Catholic decrees concerning the Immaculate Conception and the Bodily Assumption of Mary the mother of our Lord. Such decrees are not, however, regarded as introducing novelties, or as adding anything to the essential content of the faith. They are held to do no more than make finally explicit something that was from the beginning implicit in the faith, although it may have long remained unperceived; and their validity is defended on this ground as well as on that of the authority of the Church. Appeal is made, in fact, to their intrinsic value as expressive of Christian truth.

Now it must be admitted that there is no reason fundamentally why the Church should not declare some fresh formulation of Christian truth to be authoritative dogma. This was in effect done when at Nicaea and Chalcedon new forms of words were authorized for the expression of old truth in an idiom more appropriate to the needs of the time; and what was done then may very well be done again. But it cannot be rightly done unless the meaning and content of the new form of words is in undoubted and demonstrable harmony with the original gospel as this is given to us in the New Testament. Otherwise the Christian faith is in danger of being distorted and misrepresented—as in fact it must be said to be in the case of the Marian dogmas. These might conceivably be, as their apologists claim that they are, reasonable inferences from what we know, or may suppose that we know, of the part played by Mary in connexion with the Incarnation; and if they did no more than assert a miraculous beginning and ending of her life, they might be relatively innocuous. But it is by no means innocuous when the acceptance of such assertions is declared to be necessary to salvation, and when they are allowed to encourage belief in Mary as an exalted being who holds a position midway between her divine Son and ordinary mortals.

The thought of Mary as a mediatrix between us and Christ, as if we must come to Christ through her, contradicts the plain testimony of Scripture that it was by means of her that Christ came to us, and now that He has come there is no question of her further mediation. No hint can be found in the New Testament that she was anything else but an ordinary mortal, though she was undoubtedly chosen by God to be a special recipient and instrument of His gracious saving activity. It was of pure grace that the Son of God 'did not abhor the Virgin's womb', but chose that way of entry into our human life; and it was greater grace if she was an ordinary mortal than if she had been perfectly holy and sinless, for as the Immaculate there would have been nothing in her for Him to 'abhor'. Doubtless, the humanity which He took from her He purified by taking it; but it is of the essence of His grace that He does not shun contact with the sinful and unholy, but identifies Himself with them in order to redeem them. It is therefore entirely illegitimate so to separate Him from sinners that the good offices of His mother are required to mediate between men and Himself.

By the exaltation of Mary, however, not only is the grace of our Lord Jesus Christ obscured, but the true significance of Mary herself is lost. As the New Testament represents her, at any rate, Mary is far from usurping, or in any way intruding upon, the position of her Son as the one Mediator between God and men (1 Tim 2[5]). On the contrary, by the humility of her trusting and obedient response to the Word of divine grace (Lk 1[38]), she furnishes a signal example of true evangelical faith.

DOGMA AS AN AFFIRMATION OF GRACE

Hers is the faith that takes God at His Word, and sings *Magnificat* in His praise, not its own. Later in the gospel story, it is true, she appears beset with doubt and perplexity; but that too belongs to the experience of evangelical faith, and for our comfort we may recall that it is not the end of the story. Mary's faith did not finally fail, for the last thing we are told of her is that she was found among the disciples of the risen Lord (Acts 1^{14}). It is thus that Mary herself can be claimed as exemplifying evangelical faith—the faith which is centred in God and His grace alone, and which cannot accept as valid any dogmatic proposition that fails to express in one way or another that same grace.

The decisive criterion of dogmatic validity is that the formulae which are used should really express, and not distort or obscure, the truth of divine love and grace. Yet even when such validity appears to have been attained, we must beware of taking the form of words in which the truth is expressed, to be as final and absolute as the truth itself. For, as has already been said, a formula which is meaningful in one time and place can cease to be meaningful in another time and place; and we may add here, that even in the same time and place, for people with different backgrounds of thought, the same form of words can convey different meanings, and different forms of words may be needed to convey the same meaning. Failure to recognize this fact has been responsible for many evils in Christian history, and it still has much to do with the divisions between the churches. It is this fact, moreover, that underlies the criticism of the Creeds which we noted at the beginning of this chapter.

Rightly understood, the Creeds undoubtedly give expression to essential Christian truth, as we have tried to show. But they express it in terms of the thought of their day, which in the changed situation of our day are often far from readily understood. Therefore the plea that they should be restated is both legitimate and necessary—provided that restatement means no more and no less than translation into terms that will bring home their essential meaning more clearly and cogently to modern men. At the same time, it must be recognized that modern terms will possess no more finality than ancient terms; for although the truth they seek to express may be absolute, they cannot themselves be other than relative to their own time and place.

But it may be asked in conclusion, if the fundamental idea that seeks expression in Christian dogma is that of the grace and unmerited love of God, why should we not solve the whole problem of dogma by contenting ourselves with the simple affirmation that 'God is love'? This is, no doubt, the essence of the 'simple gospel' preferred by many of the critics of the Creeds, who find ecclesiastical dogma by comparison obscure, burdensome and unnecessary. But is it, after all, so certain that to say 'God is love' is really to preach a simple gospel? 'Love' is a word that can be used, as everyone knows, in many different senses, and much more is needed than the allegedly simple statement that God is love, in order to express the Christian belief about God. And the more that is needed is not simply a formal definition of the Christian idea of love; for Christian faith is not simply the acceptance of an abstract conception of the nature of God, but is rather the assertion of certain concrete events as acts of God, in which He reveals what He is by what he does. To say 'God is love', in the full Christian sense, requires us to understand that God creates, redeems, and sanctifies. Divine love is never merely an emotion or an attitude, it is active will and deed. And unless this aspect receives due recognition, then the gospel is not properly proclaimed. We must say, not simply 'God is love', but 'God so loved the world that he gave his only-begotten Son . . .' (Jn 3^{16}); and so soon as we say this, we are in the realm of dogma, as that term has been defined in the foregoing pages. What is more, if we had space to explore that realm further on the lines we have hitherto followed, we should inevitably be led to affirm that the God who is love is also Father, Son, and Holy Spirit, the eternal and ever-blessed Trinity.

SIX

Developments of the Doctrine of Grace

1 GRACE AS AN INFUSED POWER OR QUALITY

ONE OF the most important steps toward the formulation of a specific doctrine of grace was taken by the North African lawyer-theologian, Tertullian (*c.* AD 153-225), with whom the characteristically Western doctrine of original sin also took its rise. In his thought, the ideas of sin and grace are given a greater prominence and a greater depth than they had been accorded since New Testament times. But his thinking was considerably influenced by Stoic philosophy, and in particular by the Stoic idea that all existence, of whatever kind, is basically of a material nature. Even 'soul' and 'spirit' are conceived as consisting of exceedingly subtle and tenuous forms of matter, which can interpenetrate the grosser forms such as constitute bodies. God himself is actually thought of in this way, so that Tertullian can say: 'Who will deny that God is a body, even though "God is a spirit"?' This materializing view of spiritual realities furnished the background against which Tertullian interpreted biblical and traditional Christian teaching, and it affected his doctrine both of sin and of grace.

The Fall of Adam, Tertullian maintains, has resulted not only in the generally admitted curse of mortality upon the human race, but also in an inherited sinfulness, a flaw in the soul. From this *vitium originis*, or 'original fault', there has followed a 'corruption of nature', which has become 'second nature' and is transmitted from generation to generation of men by the natural processes of birth. (Tertullian holds a traducianist as opposed to a creationist view of the soul: each individual soul is not a new creation of God, but is derived together with the body from the parents. Hence, while regarding the soul as the seat of sin, it is easy for him to think of sin as transmissible by inheritance.) Alongside this idea, however, and never quite reconciled with it, stands Tertullian's insistence on the freedom of the human will to choose between good and evil, and his objection to infant baptism on the grounds that infants are 'innocent' and not yet in need of the forgiveness of sins. Nevertheless, he does not regard the innocence of infancy as capable of lasting, or the power of free will as sufficient to secure man's salvation. There is no salvation without grace.

Grace is imparted primarily through baptism, with which traditionally the forgiveness of sins and the gift of the Holy Spirit are associated. Tertullian holds that in baptism all the past sins of the baptized are forgiven, and grace is given to enable him, if he will, to avoid sin in the future. Grace is here virtually identified with the gift of the Spirit, and it is conceived, moreover, in essentially impersonal terms as a supernatural, yet quasi-material, substance or energy. This conception is no doubt mainly due to Tertullian's Stoic materialism, yet it has some points of contact with the Pauline idea of grace. Although St Paul thinks of grace primarily in terms of the activity of God, he does at times refer to it as a gift and a power, some *thing* imparted to man; and in any case, the very use of a substantive tends to suggest a substance. It is true that neither St Paul nor the New Testament generally, connects grace explicitly with the sacraments; but the sacraments are a mode of the proclamation of the Gospel, and they form a vital part of that concrete environment of grace 'wherein we stand' as Christians. Hence it is not unintelligible that Tertullian should associate grace especially with baptism, the sacrament by which men are visibly admitted to the realm of grace. But be that as it may, it is a fact that from the time of Tertullian onward, grace—at any rate saving grace—tended to be thought of as a more or less impersonal power imparted through the sacraments.

A further point of importance concerns the function of grace in the life of the believer as Tertullian conceives it. 'The force of divine grace', he says, 'is more potent than nature'; and he thinks of grace as given to man to assist his free will and overcome the corruption of his nature. It is essential, he holds, that the power of free will should be subject to grace in us if we are to be saved. With the aid of grace we must, after baptism, seek to live in obedience to God's commandments; and if at any time we fail, we must render 'satisfaction' to God for our failure. For God is a Judge, who rewards men according to their works, and even in heaven He apportions to them only such a degree of blessedness as they have merited. When He is offended, he requires satisfaction. Even the forgiveness and grace of baptism seem to be represented by Tertullian as contingent on the sufficiency of the penitence of the baptized; and for sins committed after baptism he holds that it is necessary to atone by the voluntary renunciation of something otherwise entirely lawful.

Tertullian's conception of the relation between man and God is thus fundamentally legalistic, and the conception of grace is adapted to fit this scheme. But here again there are Pauline and New Testament ideas which might seem to support his view. In Romans 6, for instance, St Paul teaches that the baptized Christian must renounce sin and devote himself to righteousness, knowing that 'the wages of sin is death'. Yet St Paul also firmly opposes grace to law and works, as Tertullian does not; for the basic contrast in Tertullian's thought is rather between grace and nature, as the foregoing account should have made sufficiently clear. This contrast, and with it the almost inevitable connexion between grace and merit, have played a part of immense importance in the history of Christian thought since Tertullian's time, and we must therefore now examine them more closely.

II GRACE CONTRASTED WITH NATURE

The contrast between grace and nature was strongly developed by St Augustine (c. AD 354-430), the theologian of grace *par excellence*, whose views found their most vigorous expression in controversy with the British monk, Pelagius (c. AD 360-420), and his followers.

As the Pelagians understood it, grace meant first of all the gift to man at his creation of reason and freewill, of which the former carried with it a knowledge of God's 'natural law', while the latter furnished the possibility of obedience to the law. The Fall of Adam did not destroy these natural powers, and Adam's descendants have inherited no corruption from him, since each individual soul is a fresh creation of God. (The Pelagians were creationist in their view of the soul, as was the Eastern Church already, and as the Western Church afterwards became.) If, therefore, there is any bias toward sin, it proceeds not from inheritance but from example, since men have become accustomed to sinning. But to counter-balance this, further grace has been furnished in the form of the 'new law', which includes the law of Moses and the teaching and example of Jesus. Moreover, through baptism all past sins are forgiven, so that men can start life afresh, as innocent as Adam before his fall; and if they will use the grace available to them, they can live without sin in obedience to God's commandments and so secure their salvation. That is what men ought to do, and it is a fundamental principle of Pelagianism that 'I ought' means 'I can'. Pelagius's disciple, Caelestius, if not Pelagius himself, appears to have held that even among the heathen, and before the coming of Christ, there were some who were sinless.

In contrast to the Pelagians, Augustine maintains that, besides reason and free will, Adam before the Fall was given an 'assisting grace'. With the aid of this grace he was 'able not to sin', and if he had never yielded to temptation he would eventually have reached a stage where he was 'not able to sin'; but through the Fall he lost the assisting grace and became 'unable not to sin'. His reason was darkened and his will perverted, so that he could scarcely any longer perceive, and could no longer pursue, the good. His lower passions thus got out of hand, and he fell a helpless victim to 'concupiscence', whereby he became subject to both spiritual and physical disintegration and death. All his descendants, moreover, suffer as a result of his fall. Since they were in Adam when he sinned, they were naturally involved in his sin and guilt. Even if each individual human soul is a fresh creation of God—a point on which Augustine never quite made up his mind—yet the soul is affected by the body in which it dwells, and the body as derived from Adam is begotten in, and therefore dominated by, concupiscence (original sin). Consequently, mankind as a whole is a 'mass of sin' and a 'mass of perdition', out of which none can be saved but by the grace of God alone.

The grace of God has been revealed through Christ, in whom God Himself has stooped down to us men in order to raise us up from the depth to which we have fallen. Augustine is prepared to speak of creation as a work of grace, as the Pelagians do, but he refuses to regard this as grace in the full and proper sense of the term. Before man was created, he says, he merited nothing and hoped for nothing—how could he when he did not exist?— and therefore we may say that it was grace by which he was created. But when man had sinned, and merited evil, and could expect only damnation, it was far greater grace by which he was redeemed. That is grace in the full and proper sense: the grace of our Lord Jesus Christ.

Grace, as Augustine understands it, depends on no merit in man. 'Grace', he says, 'is not grace unless it is given gratis.' Nor is grace appropriated by man's free will or any other power of his fallen nature. The entire appropriation of salvation is a work of grace. It begins, quite independently of any human initiative, with 'prevenient' or 'operating' grace, which produces a twofold effect. First, faith is awakened in man and a good will is given to him (i.e. a will to resist the impulses of original sin); then—and only then—his sins are forgiven and righteousness is implanted in his heart by an 'infusion of charity' (cf. Rom 5[6]). In this way man is 'justified'—and according to Augustine we may say he is justified either by faith or by love (charity). He is also ready for the next gift of grace, 'co-operating grace'. This furthers the work of the grace already given, co-operating with it so as to enable man to overcome the original sin that still remains in him and to live a life well-pleasing to God. With all this, however, a man is not yet saved;

nor has he any guarantee of final salvation, unless he receives a further degree of grace, 'irresistible grace', which imparts to him the 'gift of perseverance'. This is not given to all, even of those who receive the earlier instalments of grace, but only to those whom God has predestined for eternal salvation, and who are known to God alone.

When we turn to the medieval Schoolmen, we find a doctrine of grace which, while avoiding the extremes both of Pelagianism and Augustinianism, reflects the influence of them both. There are other influences, of course, which also play their part, and there are differences of emphasis between the different schools; but with these we need not concern ourselves here. For scholastic theology in general displays the same basic structure, and a structure in which the contrast between grace and nature is of quite fundamental importance. The way in which this contrast is understood may be illustrated as follows.

In respect of man's 'original state' before the Fall, a distinction is drawn between the natural powers with which man was created, and a supernatural gift of grace 'superadded' to them. The natural powers included reason, or intellect, and free will; and while the former of these carried with it the capacity for a certain rational knowledge of God and His law, the latter furnished the possibility of attaining to a certain level of moral virtue by obedience to the law. The 'superadded' grace, on the other hand, provided man with a supernatural 'adornment', consisting of the theological virtues of faith, hope and charity, and constituting his 'original righteousness', without which he could not be fully pleasing to God or fitted for eternal life. There was some division of opinion among the Schoolmen, as to whether the natural and the supernatural endowments of man were 'concreated' (i.e. given to him simultaneously at his creation), or whether the supernatural gift was deferred until he should have prepared himself for it by the right use of his reason and free will. But there was universal agreement that through the Fall man had forfeited supernatural grace and was left with his purely natural powers; and also that what had happened to the first man affected also his descendants, since Adam, having lost the gift of grace himself, was naturally incapable of transmitting it to his children.

It was, however, a matter of debate, whether and to what extent man's natural endowments had been impaired by the Fall, and what, if anything, fallen man could do toward securing his salvation. All the schools agreed that in order to be saved man must regain the 'adornment' of grace that Adam had lost, and that the possibility of his doing so was given through the atoning work of Christ. The question therefore was, whether and how far the natural man could avail himself of this possibility without the aid of supernatural grace. The majority of the Schoolmen, who believed that man's natural powers were undoubtedly impaired (though certainly not destroyed or totally corrupt), made no great claims for man at this point, while those who held that human nature was unimpaired claimed a very great deal. Yet even those who made the highest claims did not claim quite everything for man, since they made every man's salvation depend in the last resort on the predestinating will of God. To this point we shall have occasion to return, but here it should be noticed how this whole discussion turns on the question, how much nature must do and how much grace—or how much man and how much God—in order that man may appropriate salvation. The assumption is that whatever is done by the one cannot be done by the other; so that nature and grace, while in one sense complementary, are also mutually exclusive.

This entire conception was rejected by Luther, whose thought moves along other than scholastic—or even Augustinian—lines, despite frequent similarities of terminology. For Luther, the grace of God signifies primarily, not a supernatural energy or quality imparted to the human soul, but the gracious dealing of God Himself, quite personally, with men. And Luther's interest in men centres neither in the natural nor the supernatural qualifications which they may conceivably possess, but in their personal relationship to God. This relationship determines all their other relationships, so that where it is right, they are right, where it is wrong, they are wrong; and therefore it is quite the most important thing about them. That, at any rate, is Luther's conviction, which is reflected in every aspect of his thought, and not least in his doctrine of the Fall and original sin.

Before the Fall, as Luther sees it, man was in a relation to God that was wholly based on and governed by God's grace, to which man responded with faith. Faith, which means obedient trust (or trustful obedience), is in Luther's view the only right and proper response of man to his Maker; indeed, it is the natural response, like that of a child to his father. Man's 'original state', therefore, which was characterized by this response of faith to God's grace, was his truly natural state. It was a state in which his whole life was so centred in God, that in thought, will and action he was governed solely by the good and gracious will of God. It was as if he had 'no will of his own', no desire but to do the will of God, whose word of command and promise he implicitly believed. This was what constituted man's 'original righteousness'—the right relationship to God, and therefore to all else, for which and in which he was created. Hence, whereas for the Schoolmen man before the Fall was in a state of nature plus grace, we may say that for Luther he was in a natural state of grace.

What happened at the Fall, according to Luther, was that man fell out of his originally right relation to God into a wrong one. This came about through his being led to doubt and disbelieve God's word, and to believe another word instead, whereby he became subject to another will, alien and hostile to the divine. Inevitably, therefore, his relationship to God was wrong, and with it all his other relationships were disordered. In this state of 'original sin', moreover, all the children of Adam are begotten, and into the conditions resulting from it they are born. Since the Fall, man does not believe in, and therefore does not obey, God's will any more, for he is governed by self-will. Self, not God, is central in the life of fallen man. But this is

DEVELOPMENTS OF THE DOCTRINE OF GRACE

in the deepest sense a quite unnatural state of affairs, since in the nature of things the one and only centre of all existence must clearly be God. Hence we may say that, whereas for the Schoolmen man after the Fall is in a state of nature minus grace, for Luther he is rather in an unnatural state of disgrace.

There is, of course, nothing that man in this situation can do to put things right. Any endeavours that he may make to do so are inevitably misdirected, since they are self-centred and self-willed. Only God can save man from himself; and to this end God has taken action in Christ. In almost unbelievable grace God Himself has entered into the situation resulting from the Fall, in order by the power of His own presence and word and work to break man's bondage and lead him into the liberty of the children of God.

III GRACE COMBINED WITH MERIT

To sinful, self-centred man, the idea of either giving or getting something for nothing seems more than a little absurd: it stands to reason that there must be a *quid pro quo*. Hence the idea that God in His grace deals with men quite without regard to their deserts is difficult to grasp. Moreover, the New Testament itself, while it speaks of unmerited grace, speaks also of rewards and punishments for a life well or evilly lived. It is therefore not difficult to understand how, quite early in the history of the Church, salvation came to be regarded as a reward for merit, and grace as the means by which men were enabled to acquire merit. The notion of merit, in fact, became dangerously prevalent in popular piety, and even in a theologian like Tertullian, as we have seen, it could seriously modify the conception of grace. What is more, even St Augustine himself, who is so sure that all is of grace, can also use the language of popular piety and speak quite readily of merit. In doing so, it is true, he has no intention of suggesting that man can acquire any merit apart from grace, for he strongly insists that 'when God crowns our merits, He crowns only his own gifts'. Augustine's contemporaries and successors, however, were for the most part unwilling to go all the way with him in this, and subsequent discussion of the doctrine of grace tended to proceed on the assumption that there should be, not an identification, but a synthesis of merit and grace.

When we come to the great Franciscan Schoolmen of the thirteenth and fourteenth centuries, we find grace and merit combined in a doctrine that distinguishes between two kinds of grace and two kinds of merit. There is 'grace given gratis' and 'grace making gracious (*or* acceptable)', and there is a 'merit of congruence' and a 'condign merit' or 'merit of worthiness'. The first kind of grace is largely identified with the natural knowledge of God and His law, and the natural desire for the good, which all men as rational beings are held to possess; though sometimes it is stated to be something more—namely, an impulse supernaturally imparted to the will, to follow the light of reason and the promptings of conscience. When a man obeys such an impulse (whether it be natural or supernatural) and 'does what in him lies' to observe the requirements of the law, then he acquires the 'merit of congruence'. It is true that nothing he can do at this stage is meritorious in the strict sense of the term, yet it is congruent, or fitting, that God should recognize and reward his endeavours, and therefore we may rightly speak of a 'merit of congruence'. The reward thereby merited is the gift of 'grace making acceptable', which restores to man the 'adornment' of supernatural virtue that Adam lost at the Fall. Then, by using this grace and exercising himself in virtue, a man can acquire merit in the full and proper sense of the 'merit of worthiness', and in this way can qualify for the supreme reward of eternal life and blessedness.

The Franciscans differ as to precisely how much is implied by the phrase 'what in him lies'. Alexander of Hales (*c.* 1175-1245) and St Bonaventura (1221-74), who hold that human nature has been impaired by the Fall, claim no more than that man is able to produce an imperfect kind of penitence, faith and hope. Duns Scotus (*c.* 1266-1308) and William of Ockham (*c.* 1300-49), who believe that human nature is unimpaired, and

DEVELOPMENTS OF THE DOCTRINE OF GRACE

who especially emphasize the freedom of the human will, maintain that the natural man is capable of fulfilling all the commandments of God and loving God above all things. This is also the view of the Nominalist disciples of Scotus and Ockham, in whose theology Luther was subsequently trained. Yet all parties are agreed that there is no salvation for man without the gift of 'grace making acceptable', and those who most strongly insist on man's ability to qualify for this gift, insist just as strongly that God is in no sense obliged to give it. Everything depends on God's 'free acceptation' of man's endeavours as meritorious, and this is determined by his inscrutable, predestinating will.

A somewhat different, and more nearly Augustinian, view of the relation between grace and merit is taken by the greatest of all the Schoolmen, the Dominican St Thomas Aquinas (*c.* 1225-74). For him, there is no question of any merit prior to the gift of the grace that makes a man acceptable to God. There must, of course, be a preparation for the reception of this gift, and that is effected by a prevenient 'assisting grace', with which man's free will co-operates. But 'assisting grace' is not given to all men; and where it is given, it has nothing to do with any merit, either actual or foreseen, in the recipients. Neither is the co-operation of the human will in any way meritorious, since that also, in St Thomas's view (which is strongly predestinarian), depends ultimately on the will of God. When, however, a man is duly prepared, he receives the gift of 'grace making acceptable', or 'habitual grace' as St Thomas also calls it. This means that a new *habitus* or disposition is given to him through an 'infusion of charity', so that he regains the 'original righteousness' lost at the Fall, without which he cannot be acceptable to God or have any hope of salvation.

In connexion with 'habitual grace', St Thomas uses the Augustinian distinction between 'operating' and 'co-operating' grace, in order to represent two aspects of its working. As 'operating grace' it effects the justification of the ungodly; for it enables him to turn in true faith (not merely intellectual belief, but 'faith furnished with charity') toward God, and in true penitence (based on love of the good, and not merely on fear of punishment) away from sin, so that he qualifies for the forgiveness of sins and acceptance with God. In this way man is justified, not only in the sense of having his sins forgiven, but in the sense of being made righteous. 'Co-operating grace' then comes into action, enabling the justified man to do good works as God wills, and thereby to acquire merit.

In speaking of merit, St Thomas uses the distinction between the merit of congruence and the merit of worthiness, which we have already seen in the Franciscans. But unlike the Franciscans, he uses it only in order to distinguish between two ways of looking at the same thing. One and the same act performed in a state of habitual grace can be regarded either as the result of human volition or of divine grace. In so far as it is the former, it cannot be said to carry with it any merit in the strict sense of the term, but we may well say that it carries the merit of congruence. In so far, however, as it is the latter, it undoubtedly carries the full merit of worthiness. By means of such merits, moreover, man is able to obtain an increase of grace—and thereby to acquire more merit, so that he increasingly qualifies for eternal salvation. Yet no man can be sure (except by special divine revelation, which is very rarely given) that he is numbered among those who will in fact finally be saved. There can be no assurance of salvation, since everything depends on God's unfathomable predestination.

By contrast with the Schoolmen, Luther completely denies the possibility of any synthesis between grace and merit, and attacks the doctrine of merit root and branch. It is sometimes suggested that if Luther had been brought up on Thomistic instead of Nominalist theology, he would have reacted less violently than in fact he did against medieval Catholicism, since St Thomas clearly has a much richer doctrine of grace. That may possibly be so; but Luther would almost certainly have said that St Thomas had only brought confusion into the doctrine of grace by insisting on retaining the idea of merit, not

DEVELOPMENTS OF THE DOCTRINE OF GRACE

to mention that St Thomas's conception of grace is also in other respects different from Luther's. For Luther, salvation is by grace *alone;* not by grace plus merit, not even by grace producing merit, and certainly not by grace earned by merit. No man can ever acquire any merit in the sight of God; for we men owe to God all that we have and are, so that even if we perfectly did His will and fulfilled His commandments, He would owe us nothing. And when we have not done His will, but are disobedient sinners, and yet in spite of all He gives us Christ to redeem us, then it is nothing short of blasphemy to talk of merit. Even the carefully guarded idea of the 'merit of congruence' is impious in Luther's view. It is not for us to speculate about what it is 'fitting' for God to do, and then argue that He does it, but we must look at what God has in fact done in Christ. That is the unanswerable argument against every idea of merit.

Instead of combining grace with merit, Luther connects it exclusively with faith. Like St Paul, he believes that salvation 'is of faith, that it may be of grace'. But this means, of course, that he has a different conception of grace from that of the Schoolmen—and for that matter, a different conception of faith. We have already noticed something of the difference in considering the scholastic contrast between grace and nature, which obviously is very closely connected with the synthesis of grace and merit. But it cannot be too strongly emphasized, that when Luther insists that we are saved by grace alone, to the exclusion of merit, he is not simply asserting one aspect of scholastic doctrine while repudiating the other. Grace, as he understands it, is of such a nature that it cannot be combined with merit, but must be connected exclusively with faith. In fact, adapting St Paul's phrase, we might say that, for Luther, salvation is of faith *because* it is of grace.

IV GRACE MEDIATED SACRAMENTALLY

If we ask St Augustine, the Schoolmen and Luther, how grace comes to men, or by what specific, concrete means it is given to them, their answers will differ considerably. They will all refer us, without doubt, to the teaching and the sacramental life of the Church; but they will not all take the same view of the relation between these things and grace itself. In what follows we shall confine ourselves chiefly to a consideration of saving grace, as distinct from any lesser degree of merely preparatory grace, although preparatory grace also, except where it is regarded as a universal human endowment or as a direct interior action on the soul of the elect, may be thought to be mediated through the life and witness of the Church. It is, however, in connexion with the idea of saving grace that the differences are most marked and most instructive.

According to St Augustine, at any rate in one aspect of his thought, grace is to be found only through the word and sacraments of the Catholic Church. By the authority of the Church, men are moved to believe the gospel and to seek—in the Church—the salvation which the gospel offers. In the sacraments of the Church there is an invisible gift of saving grace bound up with a visible sign. Augustine uses the word 'sacrament' with a wide range of reference, but of chief importance to him are the sacraments of baptism and the eucharist. In baptism sins are forgiven and the gift of the Holy Spirit is imparted in the form of an 'infusion of charity'. In the eucharist this gift of grace is increased—for those who use the sacrament rightly.

Now, to use the sacrament rightly means to receive it in faith and within the fold of the Catholic Church. Augustine attaches great importance to faith, but saving faith always means for him the faith that 'worketh by charity'; and charity, as he understands it, does not exist outside the Catholic Church. Christians who cut themselves off from the Church by heresy or schism, are guilty of a denial of charity, and therefore no matter what faith they have, or how formally correct their sacraments are, it is all of no avail for their salvation. 'The sacrament', says Augustine, 'is one thing, the virtue of the sacrament another; it is one thing not to have the sacrament, another thing not to have it usefully.' Hence, the baptism of heretics may be valid (to use a modern term), so that it need not be repeated if they return to the Catholic fold; but it has certainly no saving efficacy unless and until they do so return.

At the same time, Augustine does not hold that all who are within the Catholic fold necessarily receive the gift of grace in the sacraments. There is nothing automatic about it, and even Catholics may fail to have the sacrament 'usefully'. If they have not true faith, they may well receive the visible sign of the sacrament, but they will not receive the invisible grace which it signifies. Augustine's sacramental theory is expressed in the formula, 'The Word is added to the element, and there is the sacrament'; which implies that the Word is the decisive thing, rather than the visible sign. That this is so, is confirmed by his striking saying, with reference to eucharistic participation in the Body of Christ: 'Believe, and thou hast eaten!' For one who does not believe, the physical eating will, of course, bring no benefit, but Augustine means more than this. He is prepared to say that for those who truly believe, it is possible to receive the invisible grace even without the visible sign. Indeed, he knows this is so, for hermits who have lived long years in the solitude of the wilderness are living proof of it. Grace may thus be imparted, apparently, without any outward means, directly to the human soul. Here we touch another aspect of Augustine's thought, closely connected with his Neoplatonic inheritance, which does not easily harmonize with the traditional and popular Catholicism of the aspect described above.

In another particular, also, Augustine's doctrine of grace tends to run counter to his insistence on the necessity of the Catholic Church and its means of grace for salvation. The visible, institutional Church is, for him, a 'very mixed body' of wheat and tares; that is, of those in whom the work of grace is effective, and those in whom it is not. Hence the true Church may be said to consist of the former, the 'congregation of saints', who alone have hope of salvation. Yet not all of these are certain to be saved, since grace may not work in them irresistibly to give them the 'gift of perseverance'. Only the elect, those who are predestined for it, will attain final salvation—and who these are, no man can know. We cannot even say with certainty that everyone who is predestined for salvation must necessarily be found within the fold of the Catholic Church before he dies!

It was not, however, such ideas as these that were most influential in the legacy that Augustine handed on to the Middle Ages—except among the heretical, sectarian movements, which are outside our purview here. Instead, the idea of the institutional Church as the sole purveyor of salvation became all the more firmly entrenched, and the doctrine of grace all the more firmly bound up with that of the sacraments. Indeed, the scholastic doctrine of grace and the scholastic doctrine of the sacraments are virtually the same thing, since saving grace, at any rate, is held to be given solely through the sacraments.

Already before the time of St Thomas Aquinas, the wider use of the term 'sacrament' had given place to one more restricted, and the number of the sacraments had been reduced to seven. It had also been established that the sacraments were not merely symbolical rites, but 'efficacious signs of grace', actual vehicles of grace. St Thomas develops these ideas, arguing that all seven sacraments were instituted by Christ, describing them as 'sanctifying signs', and declaring that they are effective *ex opere operato*. This last statement means that the correct performance of the sacramental rite guarantees, not only the presence and availability of grace, but also its effective operation, provided only that the recipient of the sacrament does not 'place an obstacle' (*ponere obicem*), i.e. is not in a state of soul that is actively resistant to grace. Faith on the recipient's part is, of course, necessary, except in the case of infant baptism, which presupposes the faith of the Church; and in the case of adult baptism and the sacrament of penance, penitence as well as faith is required. But faith here means little more than bare assent to the teaching of the Church.

Baptism and penance are 'justifying sacraments', which do

not require the recipient to be already in a state of grace. By baptism the 'grace that makes acceptable' is imparted, whereby the baptized receive an 'infusion of charity' and the remission of guilt both in respect of original sin and of all past actual sins. St Thomas equates this infusion of grace with the justification of the ungodly, and says that it can be described as justification either by faith or by love (charity). In the justified man, however, there remains concupiscence as a 'tinder' of sin, an ever-present incentive to sin. If by yielding to it he falls into mortal (as distinct from venial) sin, then he loses his baptismal grace and is in need of a fresh justification. But baptism, which imprints an 'indelible character' on the soul, is unrepeatable; therefore he must turn to the sacrament of penance, coming in penitence to confess his sin and receive absolution from the priest. In this way the guilt of his mortal sin can be blotted out, so that he is delivered from the liability to eternal punishment. The liability to temporal punishment, however, remains; that is to say, the obligation to carry out acts of 'satisfaction' prescribed (partly as a deterrent from further sin) by the priest or other ecclesiastical authority. Failure to fulfil this obligation is punished by God, either on earth or in Purgatory, unless it is remitted by means of an 'indulgence'.

There was much debate among the Schoolmen as to the degree of penitence required for the effective reception of absolution. Some held that attrition, or the penitence arising from fear, was sufficient; others, that contrition, arising from love of the good and hatred of sin, was necessary. But how could a man produce contrition when he was not in a state of grace? Or if he could produce it, where was the need for him to do penance, in view of the traditional teaching of the Church that true repentance itself obtained immediate divine forgiveness? St Thomas answers here that the grace of the sacrament itself, operating so to speak in advance, produces contrition in those intending to do penance; and it is not pointless for them still to do it, since through confession and absolution they will receive an increase of the grace obtained by their contrition. But this does not exempt them from the obligation to make satisfaction, or from the threat of severer penalties in Purgatory if they fail to fulfil it. Most men may expect to suffer in Purgatory, both for failures in this respect and for venial sins not remitted before they die. Yet the Church has the means by which to lighten temporal punishments. It can grant indulgences; and it can do so, according to St Thomas—who here follows the lead of Alexander of Hales—by drawing on the superabundant 'treasury of merit' furnished by Christ and the saints. What is more, even for souls in Purgatory, indulgence may be secured by the intercession of the Pope.

The only other sacrament that we need notice here is that of the eucharist, which by this time has become the sacrifice of the Mass. This sacrament requires that those who wish to participate in it should not be in a state of mortal sin. The grace of the eucharist deals only with the guilt of venial sins (which it may, however, prevent from becoming mortal sins). It renews and increases the 'infusion of charity' received through the justifying sacraments, of which the effect is weakened by venial sins, and it thus transforms attrition once more into contrition. The grace of the eucharist, however, extends its operation far beyond the circle of communicants. For the sacrament is a sacrifice, a 'representative image of the passion of Christ' and an unbloody repetition of the sacrifice of Golgotha, which is offered to God for the obtaining of blessings both material and spiritual. It can be offered on behalf of the absent as well as those present, and on behalf of the dead as well as the living—on the assumption that they have some measure of faith. This conception of the eucharistic sacrifice is, of course, largely bound up with the doctrine of transubstantiation, officially confirmed by the Lateran Council of 1215, according to which the bread and wine of the eucharist undergo a metaphysical change when they are consecrated by the priest, so that they become the very body and blood of Christ.

Now between all this and the reforming outlook of Luther there is a whole world of difference. As is well known, he

DEVELOPMENTS OF THE DOCTRINE OF GRACE 93

repudiates the idea of transubstantiation, denounces the sacrifice of the Mass, abolishes the sacrament of penance, and denies that confirmation, marriage, ordination and extreme unction are sacraments, even though there is a proper place and use for them. Of the seven sacraments he retains only two, baptism and the eucharist, or the Lord's Supper; and these he interprets very differently from the Schoolmen, in harmony with his different conception of grace.

Luther conceives of the relation between God and man, as we have already said, in an essentially personal way. For this reason, the supreme means of grace is in his view the Word of God rather than the sacraments. Indeed, he goes so far as to say that 'the Word alone is the vehicle of grace'. It is through the Word that the Holy Spirit is imparted, and through the Word alone that the sacraments have their significance. Luther can accept Augustine's definition: 'The Word is added to the element, and there is the sacrament.' He can also echo his 'Believe, and thou hast eaten!'; for still more strongly than Augustine he emphasizes the importance of faith. Here, however, it is important to remember that the Word, as Luther understands it, is always ultimately the Word that became flesh in the person of Jesus Christ. It is this Word that forms the essential content of the Scriptures and Christian preaching, through which we now encounter Christ, and which for that reason can themselves be called the Word of God; and it is this same Word that forms the essential content of the sacraments. If the Word 'added to the element' is primarily the dominical 'words of institution', it must not be forgotten that these are spoken by the incarnate Word, and are a concentrated expression of the Good News of God that He brings to us in His own person.

Nevertheless—or rather, therefore—Luther can make use of the scholastic description of the sacraments as 'efficacious signs of grace'. He does not believe that grace is given only through the sacraments, or that any special kind of grace is given through them; yet they are very far from superfluous. Consisting as they do of visible signs attached to the spoken Word, they are characteristic of the way in which God deals with men —the way that is exemplified supremely in the Incarnation itself. In the sacraments, as in the Incarnation, God shows that He wills to meet us on our own level, in and through the concrete environment of our ordinary, mundane, sin-stained existence. The water of baptism and the bread and wine of the eucharist are signs of the presence of the incarnate God in our midst, and means of His gracious dealing with us. Although no metaphysical change takes place in the elements, and no supernatural virtues are infused into us, yet when water or bread and wine are sacramentally 'in use', according to Christ's institution, then they are means which God Himself has appointed for His meeting with men. There is no question here of an *opus operatum*, a rite performed in order to influence God and obtain blessings from Him, but the sacraments are *opera Dei*, works of God, who through them seeks to influence men and get them to trust and obey His Word.

In both sacraments the words of institution contain the gracious promise of pardon and acceptance with God, which we are invited to believe. But baptism is the foundation sacrament, the sacrament of prevenient grace. It is 'God's outstretched hand, ever ready to draw us to Himself', and 'a Deluge of grace'. When the water of baptism flows over us, it is a sign that our sins are forgiven and we are accepted; but it is also a sign of our obligation daily to die to sin and rise to newness of life. The whole life of the Christian is, in fact, according to Luther, a daily baptism, a daily fulfilment of all that our baptism means; and this is a process never completed in this life, but only when through actual death and resurrection we are delivered from this sinful world and come to heaven. Nevertheless, God's covenant which He has concluded with us in our baptism, always stands firm, and the grace of baptism cannot be lost. If we fail to do our part, if we are faithless and fall into sin, we need no 'sacrament of penance' to replace our baptism, though we certainly need to repent. God, who gave us our baptism, is faithful despite our faithlessness, and does not withdraw His gift: we cannot become unbaptized, and we can always be sure of acceptance when we return in penitence to God. This does not mean, of course, that we may not need help in seeking to return, and Luther retains confession and absolution as part of the ministry of the Word—of which the sacraments themselves are indeed also a part.

There is no need to deal in detail here with the sacrament of the Lord's Supper, or 'the Mass' as Luther still calls it. It is sufficient to point out that for him the Mass is a concentrated expression of the Gospel, in which the covenant given once for all in baptism is repeatedly renewed. It is not a sacrifice, offered by us to God, but a 'testament', a legacy or gift provided for us by God; and although the elements are not transubstantiated, yet they are infallible signs of the real presence of Christ, and of God in Christ, in all the fullness of His redeeming grace.

Luther's conception of the sacramental mediation of grace differs fundamentally from that of both the Schoolmen and St Augustine. The reason for this is that for him the whole significance of the sacraments is determined by his understanding of grace. For the Schoolmen, on the other hand, the doctrine of grace is determined by the significance they attach to the traditional sacramental system of the Church. As for Augustine, we have already seen how he makes the sacraments dependent on the Church, in that he denies them any saving efficacy outside it. By contrast, Luther makes the very existence of the Church dependent on the work of divine grace through the Word and sacraments of the gospel, which itself is the power of God unto salvation.

V GRACE AND FREE WILL

All the great theologians of grace have tended to arrive in the end—if they have not started from it in the beginning—at a doctrine of predestination. It is almost inevitable that they should do so, since the more they make our salvation dependent on God and His grace, the less they leave to be done by us and our free will. This is too large and complicated a subject to take up in any detail here, but there are a number of points that should be borne in mind in order to avoid misunderstanding.

In the first place, it should be observed that there is more than one doctrine of predestination. Some of its exponents seek to rationalize the idea and reduce the offence of it, by arguing that God predestines men to salvation or perdition according to His foreknowledge of their eventual response to His grace. Others will have nothing of this, but insist that election and reprobation are determined by God without reference to the foreseen merit or faith of men, for reasons which He has not revealed to us, but which we must believe to be perfectly just. Yet even among such thoroughgoing predestinarians as these—among whom Augustine, Aquinas, Luther, and Calvin must be numbered—there are important differences. Interesting evidence of this is furnished by the fact that in some cases the doctrine of predestination is a ground of confidence and hope, in others a source of uncertainty. Augustine and Aquinas, for instance, maintain that there can be no assurance of salvation, since no man can know for certain whether or not he is among the elect—unless he receives a special revelation, which is very rare. Luther and Calvin, on the other hand, do not hesitate to preach assurance—on the basis of God's revelation of Himself in Christ. Calvin believes that through the inward witness of the Holy Spirit, the faith of the elect is marked by a certainty that is not given to the reprobate, who may well have faith, and may show the fruit of the Spirit in their lives, but have not the gift of perseverance.

At the same time, Calvin maintains a severely logical theory about God's 'eternal decree', by which the final destiny of every individual soul is irrevocably fixed; and this is an idea that can easily lead to uncertainty and despair in those in whom the witness of the Spirit is not very clear or strong. Luther, who is a little more reserved than Calvin in what he says of God's 'hidden', predestinating will, counsels those who are troubled at the thought of predestination to take refuge in 'the wounds of Christ'—as he himself was advised to do by John Staupitz long ago. There, in Christ crucified, we see the revealed will of God, which is a will to save; and there, at the foot of the Cross, every penitent believer may be assured that he is among the predestined and the elect. The difference between Luther and Calvin might be expressed thus: while Calvin says that all is of grace, but grace is not for all, Luther says both that all is of grace and grace is for all, though not all are for grace.

The second point to be noticed is that the doctrine of predestination is by no means the same thing as determinism or fatalism. From one point of view, it is essentially an assertion (however confusingly expressed) that the God of grace revealed in Christ is in supreme control, so that all things are in a heavenly Father's hands and all things work together for good. From this point of view, both Luther and Calvin denounce as heathenish all notions of luck or chance or fate, and deride the deterministic superstition of astrology. Nevertheless, there are forms of the doctrine of predestination that are hard put to it to avoid determinism; and this is particularly so where the grace of God is understood in terms of the contrast between nature and grace, or nature and supernature. In terms of that contrast, as we have seen, the divine and the human are mutually exclusive, at least in the sense that any part played by either of them in salvation inevitably diminishes the part played by the other. Hence, if all is of grace, it would seem that there is no part left for nature to play—a view which can obviously have serious practical consequences in the shape of religious and ethical indifferentism. This may partly explain why the notion of merit was so persistently retained by men like Augustine and Aquinas, who have no doubt that all is of grace. There must be some part for nature to play.

But if we think in terms of personal relationships, as Luther fundamentally does, then there need be no such mutual exclusiveness as we have just described. The activity of God by no means excludes human activity as such, but only independent, self-willed human activity. This is all that Luther means to exclude when he denies the freedom of man's will in matters relating to salvation. He wishes, he says, that the term 'free will' had never been invented, for it is not scriptural and it is very misleading. It suggests an independence man does not possess, and an initiative he has no right to claim, in his dealings with God. It was man's satanically inspired desire to show that he had a will of his own, that brought about the Fall and put man radically in the wrong with God. What men call free will is nothing else but self-will, which is admittedly free in the sense of being emancipated from God, but not in the sense of being in a position of neutrality between God and the devil so that it can equally well choose between them. On the contrary, the will of fallen man is a will that has fallen victim to the devil and is in bondage to the devil; that is, to the potent and subtle spirit of self-interest and self-concern that is precisely the mark of man's fallenness. It is this spirit that ultimately determines all that fallen man wills, and not least his endeavours to please God and set himself right with God (i.e. his religion). Hence salvation, which means precisely the putting right of the relationship that has gone wrong, must be God's work alone, and man must be 'purely passive with respect to God'.

Theological passivity, however, does not mean psychological paralysis and has nothing to do with the moral and spiritual indolence of quietism. It means that men no longer act on their own initiative, but only as they are acted upon by God; and this does not reduce them to automata, mere impersonal things, since God acts upon them in an essentially personal way, namely through His Word, which requires a response from them. The Word, moreover, always evokes a response, whether of acceptance and faith or of rejection and unbelief. That is to say, it either hardens them in their self-willed alienation from God, or it overcomes and breaks their self-will by reconciling them to God and His will. Why it does not always win the response of faith is a mystery to which only God knows the answer—the mystery of predestination.

At this point we may observe, thirdly, that the kind of problem

DEVELOPMENTS OF THE DOCTRINE OF GRACE

which gives rise to the idea of predestination occurs also in other connexions. Why is it, for instance, that of two brothers, brought up in the same environment, one becomes a convinced Communist, the other a convinced anti-Communist? When we want to explain such things, we usually refer to some influence or other that has acted upon the persons concerned and has conditioned their attitude to life. If we cannot find a satisfactory explanation on those lines, we may perhaps shrug the matter off by saying: 'There's no accounting for tastes, but it's a free country, and people have a right to their own opinions'; but we do not as a rule think of referring to their 'free will'. Indeed, sometimes we speak as if a person's own choice or decision did not enter in at all, as, for instance, when we say that an idea or a passion has 'got hold of' a man or 'got into him'—or even that it has 'bitten' him. Yet we can still hold him responsible for what he does, and we have no thought of denying his freedom—so long as no coercion or undue pressure has been brought to bear on him. Hence at this level we can say two things with equal truth. We can say—to take the example of the convinced Communist—that he is a Communist both because he believes in Communism and wishes to be a Communist, and because Communism impresses and convinces him—or, to put it in the passive, because he is impressed and convinced by Communism.

But there is a deeper aspect of the problem than this, which may be illustrated as follows. When a person is so much under the influence of another that in thought and speech and action he simply echoes and reflects the other, we may sometimes say that he 'hasn't a mind of his own', though we do not question his freedom so long as he is acting voluntarily and as he wishes to act. But if we tell such a person that it is not good for him to be so dependent on the other, and that he ought to have a mind of his own, we may well find that that is much more easily said than done. Indeed, our saying it may furnish the first incentive he has had to try to do it, and may help him to do it. On the other hand, he may resent our good advice and refuse all the more stubbornly to be emancipated from the influence we deplore. Even if he does not, he may need a great deal of counsel and help before he comes really into possession of a mind of his own and so is really free. In such a case as this, it is of course most important that the man should not become so dependent on his counsellor and helper that he simply exchanges one state of unfreedom for another. In relation to each other, human beings are meant to have minds of their own, and it is not good that one should be enslaved to another, passively carrying out the will of another, even if he likes it because he is too indolent or incompetent to think for himself. But in relation to God the position is obviously different. Here men have no right to have minds of their own or wills of their own; for that means a will emancipated from God and enslaved to the devil of self-will, in whose willing service men imagine themselves to be free. Nothing but the Word of God can reveal to them their unfreedom and bring them the help they need to set them free; yet when the Word is preached, while some are liberated, others remain all the more firmly bound. Why is it that not all accept God's message of grace?

A final word should perhaps be added here, to point out that, while the greatest theologians of grace have been strong predestinarians, at least one great preacher of grace was not. John Wesley strongly opposed the Calvinistic doctrine of predestination as it was taught in his time, and proclaimed himself an 'Arminian'. This did not mean that he had no doctrine of predestination at all, for he found one in the Bible; but he rationalized it by saying that men were predestined according to God's foreknowledge of their response to the gospel, that is, their faith or unbelief. He further maintained that, by the prevenient grace of God,[1] all men possessed at least sufficient freedom of will to enable them, if they would, to accept the gospel in faith, or perhaps we might rather say, to receive the gift of saving faith that was offered to them in the gospel. As Wesley saw it—and who can deny that he was right?—Calvin's

---

[1] Given proleptically to all men from Adam onward, on the basis of the atoning work of Christ.

doctrine limited and indeed distorted the grace of God revealed in Christ, when it taught that the gospel was to be preached to all men, yet some men by God's own decree were incapable of accepting it. Calvin's doctrine at this point reminds one of the Gnostics who, in the time of the Early Church, taught that some men were by nature incapable of salvation, while others were capable of it in differing degrees. Against this idea the Fathers of the Church protested with vigour, and men like Origen and Irenaeus asserted most strongly the freedom of the human will, which meant for them the possibility of man's receiving the salvation of God. In the time of the Reformation, however, the freedom of the human will had come to mean, not simply receptivity, but man's ability to make an active contribution to his salvation in the form of merit; and against this the Reformers protested by asserting the bondage of man's will.

SEVEN

The Reality of Grace

IN THE preceding chapters we have been chiefly concerned with the idea of grace in biblical and historical theology. We have described a variety of ways in which this idea can find expression, and outlined differing views as to its precise meaning and content. In this concluding chapter we shall attempt to consider the reality of grace in our human experience. We have seen that grace is to be understood as a manifestation of the love of God, which, while it is found at its deepest and clearest in Christ, is closely associated in traditional Christian thought with the Church, and can even be connected with Creation. In what follows, therefore, we shall try to see how, as a matter of empirical, or perhaps rather, existential fact, the gracious activity of divine love is to be perceived in Creation, in Christ, and in the Church.

I GRACE IN CREATION

Let us look first at the fact of creation, and our own creation in particular. If anything is certain about this, it is that we ourselves had nothing to do with it. Not one of us, from the first man that ever was, to the latest child born today, has brought himself into existence, or equipped himself with such powers of body and mind as he possesses. Still less have we provided the vast and varied resources of the world in which our life is set. No doubt our parents had something to do with our coming into the world; but their part was hardly more than instrumental. Parents are not creators. If they were, we should not find that some who long for children do not have them, while others have them who do not want them. The life of all of us, therefore, is a gift that none of us has done anything to achieve or deserve. We are not our own idea: we did not beget or

THE REALITY OF GRACE

conceive or bear ourselves, but we were begotten, conceived and born. For long enough afterwards we could not fend for ourselves; and when at last we could, it was only by means of abilities and resources provided for us. Hence we owe, quite literally, everything to a power not ourselves, to God.

But how do we pay our debt? How do we requite God for His gifts? By loving Him with all our heart and mind and soul and strength? By imitating His generosity and loving our neighbour as ourselves? We ought to do so surely, out of sheer gratitude to Him. But we are strangely perverse. For although we despise ingratitude shown toward a human benefactor, we are all too often quite oblivious of our ingratitude to God. Again and again we take His gifts without a word or a thought of thanks. We take them for granted, as if they belonged to us by right. We exploit them for our own ends, not asking for what purpose they were given; and instead of serving one another with them in love, we are prepared to use—or rather abuse—them in order to exploit one another and even to destroy one another. When by means of them we achieve some success, we quickly become boastful and proud, quite forgetting that we could have done nothing at all, had not our abilities and resources, and even the incentive to use them, been given to us. Yet if we do not have success, or if some gift that we value is taken away from us, then we are quick to complain and protest, as if an undoubted injustice had been done to us. We are most unreasonably apt to be pleased with ourselves when things go well with us, and displeased with God when they do not.

Our human race has clearly every reason to be ashamed of itself. We have really no excuse for our ingratitude, our ungracious response to the creating grace of God. The argument sometimes advanced, that we did not ask to be born, cannot excuse it; for we would all much rather be alive than dead. Even when in our gloomier moments we wish, like Moses or Elijah, that we were dead, or like Jeremiah and Job, that we had never been born, all that we really wish is that we were out of the particular difficulty or distress that we happen to be in at the moment. At all events, we generally employ all our ingenuity to preserve and prolong our life; and if we hear of some unhappy person who has died by his own hand, we feel that the balance of his mind must have been seriously disturbed. In any but the most abnormal circumstances it seems quite unnatural to us not to want to live. And it is just as unnatural not to be grateful for the life that we have been given.

If sometimes we are tempted to question whether there is anyone to be grateful to, we might well ask ourselves whether our doubt is not itself a symptom of ungrateful pride and subtle self-conceit. For either our life is a gift of God, who knew what he was doing when he gave it to us, or it is a product of blind, insensate forces, that had no notion of what they were producing; and in that case we are wiser and better than our maker, in spite of all our faults. But we can hardly be said to suffer from an excess of modesty if we seriously believe that that is so.

Not that when we profess belief in God we are necessarily much better than when we do not. For we can acknowledge the existence and the power and wisdom and goodness of our Creator without in the least recognizing the reality of his grace. Knowing that he is to be reckoned with, we can devote ourselves very religiously to what we regard as his service, while in fact we are serving ourselves. All too often our religion is little else but an attempt to curry favour with God, to get on the right side of Him in the hope of getting something out of Him. Even when it is highly spiritual, it can be motivated by self-concern and self-conceit rather than by loving gratitude to God. There is no less self-concern when our aim in religion is to secure our own eternal welfare, than when we seek earthly, temporal benefits; and it is just as self-conceited to think that our own moral and spiritual achievements will commend our cause to God, as to imagine that His favour can be purchased by material offerings and sacrifices. As if God were not eternally gracious, and would not give us eternal life as freely as He has given us our temporal life—if only we were willing to accept a gift!

It is true, of course, that the genuine service of God, in grateful trust and obedience, is productive of moral and spiritual excellences and leads to eternal blessedness. But these are results, not motives, in true religion; and where they are regarded as motives, religion becomes corrupt, because the relation between man and God is no longer what it ought to be.

Yet God has immense patience and forbearance with us. There would be nothing unreasonable or unjust in it if He were to say, in effect: 'I am tired of these human creatures of mine. They are an ungrateful lot; they neither trust Me nor obey Me. They turn My world into a bedlam; and now, with the scientific resources I have given them, they are threatening to blow it to pieces. They deserve no further consideration; I will withdraw My gifts from them and let them perish.' But God does not do that. As Jesus points out, He lets His sun shine and His rain fall on the just and the unjust, and he is kind to the unthankful and the evil (Mt 5^{45}, Lk 6^{35}). If He were to blot out the sunlight and withhold the rain, we should soon perish; but these basic necessities of life, and much else besides, He continues to provide in spite of the ingratitude of men and their disastrously selfish misuse of His gifts.

More than once, Jesus seeks to make us aware of the revelation of God's love and grace that is plain to see in the world around us, if only we were not so taken up with ourselves and our own affairs that we have no eyes for it. For Him as for the Psalmist, 'the heavens declare the glory of God, and the firmament sheweth his handiwork' (Ps 19^1); but He sees more deeply than the Psalmist into the nature of the divine glory, for He sees it to be the glory of eternally giving and forgiving love. In the instance just quoted, He points us to the undiscriminating character of this love, as an example of the way in which we ought to love if we would be, as we are meant to be, truly children of God. But He can also point us to the care of that same divine love for creatures far less significant, like the wild birds and wild flowers (Mt 6$^{25-33}$), as a rebuke to our anxious care for ourselves and our doubt and distrust of God.

But here the objection may be raised: 'It is all very well to talk about the blessings of the sun and the rain, but what about the disastrous droughts and floods they can cause? And while it can be very charming to contemplate the birds and flowers, what about plagues and earthquakes and poisonous reptiles and typhoid and cancer and all the other major and minor causes of human pain and misery and death? Are these, too, supposed to be evidences of the love of God?' These are questions that cannot be simply dismissed nor ought they to be too easily answered. There is clearly no unmistakable revelation of God's love in a great many things that enter into our human experience.

It could, of course, be argued that such things are not native to God's creation, but are results of the 'Fall', that is to say, they are disharmonies in the created order, resulting from the sin of man and the malice of the devil. A good case could be made out for this view, so long as we avoid taking a superficial, moralistic view of sin, or a naïvely mythological view of Satan. But that is too far-reaching a subject for us to enter into here. Instead, let us admit that the witness of creation, as we know it, to the love and grace of God is not a little ambiguous. At the same time, let us not jump too hastily to conclusions on that score. In view of the fact that a very great deal of the misery in the world is unquestionably due to human selfishness and sin, it is more than a little presumptuous for us men to sit in judgement on our Maker. What is more, there is other evidence that ought to be taken into account, besides the evidence of creation, with regard to the reality of the love and grace of God.

II GRACE IN CHRIST

Jesus Christ was as well aware as any modern man of the many aspects of our human experience that seem quite flagrantly to contradict the love of God. He was far from blind to the suffering and misery brought to men by sickness, poverty, ignorance, and their own or others' selfishness; and He saw these things more starkly than we usually do today, inasmuch as there were then far fewer agencies for the relief of pain and distress. He knew too, the dire possibilities of plague, earthquake, famine, revolution, persecution, and war. He speaks of these things in the Gospels, and He knows that they can be a severe trial to faith.

Yet He offers us no theodicy, makes no attempt to justify the ways of God to men. Behind much both of sin and of suffering He sees the working of Satanic power, and it may be legitimate to infer that for Him all evil whatsoever is ultimately traceable to this source. But why there should be a source of evil at all in God's world, He nowhere seeks to explain. That in itself is a sign that He takes evil seriously, holding it to be a real, and not merely an apparent, contradiction of God and His love, so that it cannot and must not be rationalized away. At the same time, the the problem of evil never blinds Him, as it so oftens blinds us, to the evidences of God's love, which for Him is a far deeper and more ultimate reality than all that contradicts it.

What is more, Jesus not only speaks about God's love, but He lives it. He practises what He preaches. Divine love is no mere theory for Him, but His whole life is a manifestation of it. He lives in unqualified trust and obedience toward God as His heavenly Father, and in the unreserved, selfless service of men which is the Father's will. The Synoptic record abundantly bears out the Johannine witness that He does not seek his own glory (Jn 8[50]), and that he does nothing of His own accord, but only what He sees the Father doing (Jn 5[19, 30]). Thus he fulfils the twofold commandment that sums up all the commandments: 'Thou shalt love the Lord thy God with all thy heart and with all thy mind and with all thy soul and with all thy strength; and thou shalt love thy neighbour as thyself.' In so doing, He devotes his whole energy, not to theorizing about the problem of evil, but to counteracting and overcoming evil. His 'mighty works' of compassion that restore life and health to men's bodies and minds, His authoritative words of forgiveness that release souls from the oppression of guilt and fear, His disregard of His own reputation in making Himself 'a friend of publicans and sinners'—these things are nothing else but demonstrations of the divine love in which He so passionately believes.

Jesus has come, He says, 'to call sinners' (Mk 2^{17}). That is how He understands God's love. God loves sinners—a thing unheard of in any other religion, as that acute second-century critic of Christianity, Celsus, observed. But Celsus, as his Christian opponent, Origen, pointed out, had simply never considered the possibility of a love that was not self-centred, that did not seek its own, but another's good. The same point arises also in modern times. When a Christian missionary known to the writer was addressing a Muslim audience, and spoke of the love of God for sinful men, there was a murmur of protest against such blasphemous nonsense, and an angry voice exclaimed: 'To say that God loves sinners is as absurd as saying that I like bad apples!'

It was something of the same idea that underlay the hostility of many of Jesus's contemporaries to Him. His preaching and practice of divine love toward sinners seemed to them to spell the ruin of all religion and morality. It was utterly irrational. What reason could men have for seeking to obey the will of God if they did not have to do it in order to win His regard? Or how could one revere a God who had so little regard for His own holiness and righteousness as to admit the unholy and unrighteous into His presence? It was an attitude of the kind expressed in these questions that drove Jesus to His Cross.

Jesus could have escaped the Cross if He had been willing either to abandon or drastically to modify His misssion of calling sinners. If He had said that God in His love had sent Him to convert sinners into good and righteous Pharisees, he would have aroused little or no opposition. Or if He had so thrown in his lot with sinners as to make light of sin, as if in God's sight it simply did not matter, then also He would have avoided crucifixion, since no one would have taken Him seriously. But He could do none of these things. If He had taken any other course than He actually did, He would have denied all that He knew and believed about God. He proclaimed both by His words and His actions the divine love that forgives sins; and to forgive is something quite different from treating sin as a matter of no importance: it is to recognize sin for precisely the evil that it is, and yet to refuse to let it be a barrier to fellowship with the sinner.

God's love certainly does not mean for Jesus a sentimental, easy-going tolerance of evil. He knows that there is a very stern side to God's character: the heavenly Father is also the Lord and Judge of men. This is illustrated in the parables, where a lord and master orders drastic punishment for his rebellious subjects and unfaithful servants (Mk 12^9, Mt 18$^{33-5}$, Lk 19$^{26-7}$); where invited guests who treat his invitation lightly, or respond to it too late, are irrevocably excluded from his presence (Mt 25$^{11-12}$, Lk 13$^{25-7}$, 14^{24}); or where those who find themselves on the left hand at the Last Judgement are consigned to perdition (Mt 25$^{41-6}$; cf. Mk 9$^{42-8}$). Here the principle applies, 'From him that hath not, even that which he hath shall be taken away', and we are warned of an 'outer darkness' that awaits the unfaithful and unworthy (Mt 25$^{29-30}$). The love of God, which is seen at its deepest in the grace of our Lord Jesus Christ, is 'hot with wrath' toward sin, and where sin will not yield to love, the result cannot but be disastrous for the sinner.

But the sin that will not yield to love is found by Jesus much less in those whom the scribes and Pharisees call 'publicans and sinners' than in the scribes and Pharisees themselves. It is to these, the righteous who have no need of repentance (Lk 15^7), the whole who have no need of a physician (Mk 2^{17}), that his sternest and most condemnatory words are addressed. Admittedly they are free from the sinful self-indulgence of the Prodigal Son, but they can certainly not be acquitted of the sinful self-righteousness of the Elder Brother. They are unforgiving, and they are guilty of the sin that is unforgivable because it will not be forgiven; they recognize neither their own need of forgiveness nor God's will to forgive. As the scribes and Pharisees saw it, God's will meant strict justice and the letter of the law; and it was their zeal for God's will as they understood it, that made them the bitterest enemies of Jesus, who understood God's will very differently. It was Pharisaic zeal for the law that was chiefly responsible for bringing Him to His Cross.

In the Cross of Christ the whole problem of evil is concentrated. Both the evil of sin and the evil of suffering are here seen at their worst. The sufferer is wholly innocent of the charges on which He is put to death, and those responsible for His suffering are wholly convinced that they are doing right in putting Him to death. The tragedy of the Cross lies less in the cruelty of it, and less even in the miscarriage of justice that it represents, than in the underlying repudiation by good and godly men of a goodness and godliness that transcends their own. As Jesus in His prayer for them declares: 'They know not what they do' (Lk 23[34]).

Yet the Cross of Christ is not usually thought of as a tragedy or as a symbol of evil, but as the supreme demonstration of divine love and grace. For here, in the midst of the evil that is only too evident, the love of God in which Jesus believed and by which He lived, is even more evident. He accepted the Cross in obedience to the loving will of God, refusing to adapt Himself to the loveless ways and values of men, even though He might thereby have saved His life. He went to the Cross, not (as some theories of the Atonement teach) in order to satisfy justice and set mercy free to work, but because He would not desist from preaching and practising a love that transcends all justice. He died on the Cross, not in order to persuade or enable God to forgive men's sins, but because God does forgive—in the way that Jesus forgave, when He made Himself a 'friend of publicans and sinners'.

That, at any rate, is what Jesus Himself believed about the love of God, and in Him the love that He preached was a living incarnate reality. It was love in action, the helping, healing, saving action which is grace, and it was beyond question in action in Jesus Himself. What is more, it is still a living reality. The story of Jesus did not end with His death and burial, and the love that was in action in Him is still in action in the Christian Church.

III GRACE IN THE CHURCH

If death had been the end of the story, it could only have meant that Jesus was mistaken in all that He had believed and taught about the love of God. It would have shown that God (unless He was indifferent to the whole affair) was on the side, not of Jesus, but of those who crucified Him. But in that case we could not possibly claim that the love which was an undeniable reality in Jesus was a reality also in God. We might, indeed, never have heard of Jesus, unless perhaps as a martyr for a sublime but hopeless cause. Certainly no one would have preached about Him as His disciples afterwards did; no page of the New Testament would have been written, nor any Christian sacrament celebrated; and there would therefore have been no Christian Church. Hence the very existence of the Church is evidence that death did not have the last word, and that the grace of our Lord Jesus Christ is one with the love of God.

For when Jesus of Nazareth was crucified, dead, and buried, it looked like the final defeat of all that He had believed in and lived for. From the point of view of His disciples, who had given Him their loyalty and placed all their hopes in Him, it was unrelieved disaster. The man whom they had believed to be sent from God, the appointed agent of God, had been arrested, tried (after a fashion), and executed by hanging on a cross. This meant for them that He had been repudiated by God and was under the curse of God, since the Scripture said: 'He that is hanged is accursed of God' (Deut 21^{23}; cf. Gal 3^{13}). They were in consequence baffled, disillusioned, despairing men. No one who thinks and feels himself into their situation can possibly doubt that. Yet within only a short time afterwards they were preaching the gospel of His grace, and facing for His sake ignominy and death such as He had faced for them. They were able to do this because, and only because, they were utterly convinced that He had been raised from the dead and was triumphantly alive; which meant that God had not in fact disowned Him, but on the contrary had vindicated Him.

It is true that we have no incontrovertible proof that the disciples of Jesus were right in their belief that He had risen from the dead. But there are many, and among them the most important, things in life that are beyond the possibility of incontrovertible proof, and we do not ask for it. We take whatever evidence we possess, and make up our minds; and that is what we must do here. Only those totally ignorant of the kind of men the disciples of Jesus were, and of the meaning of the things they said about Him, will be able to believe they were perpetrating a hoax when they asserted that He had risen from the dead. They quite certainly believed He had really died and been buried, and that He had really come out of the tomb alive. How this happened, they do not attempt to tell us, for none of them saw it; but they assure us that they both saw and heard and touched Him after it happened. Was this an hallucination, a case of sense-perception without sensory stimuli? Even supposing it was, we still have to face the question why it happened, why it convinced them that God had vindicated Jesus and 'made him both Lord and Christ' (Acts 2^{36}), and still more, why their conviction has come to be shared by the ever-growing numbers of the universal Church.

It really strains credulity less to believe that the conviction that Jesus Christ was alive was produced by the living Christ Himself, than to accept any other explanation. The difficulties we often feel about believing this have, of course, very little to do with the nature of the evidence. They arise almost entirely from the fact that the resurrection of Christ is a unique event, which we cannot fit into the categories of our ordinary thinking. But it is a quite unwarrantable assumption that because this kind of thing does not ordinarily happen, therefore it could never happen. If we assume that, we only show that we know neither the Scriptures nor the power of God (Mk 12^{24}). If God could make the world and give us life, why is it incredible that He should raise the dead? And if, so far, He appears to have done it only once, may we not suppose He has good reason for that? Must we always be wiser than our Maker, and prescribe for Him what He can and cannot do?

Or let us put the problem another way. If Jesus of Nazareth had been a bad man, or if resurrection from the dead were a bad thing, then it would be reasonable enough to hold that God could not have done it. But inasmuch as life is better than death, and Jesus was better than His enemies, does not the problem of evil become more acute if we deny the resurrection? For then we must say either that God is indifferent to goodness—in which case He is a demon; or else that He is powerless to save it from destruction—in which case He is simply not God. Not that the resurrection by itself, as an isolated event, would be of any great significance. The bare fact of a dead man's having come to life again, even if it could be proved beyond doubt, would not mean what the Christian faith understands by the resurrection of Jesus Christ. The resurrection of Jesus Christ means the triumph of incarnate love over the worst and final evil of the world, which is death itself.

It is the unanimous testimony of the Christian Church from the beginning, not simply that God raised Jesus Christ from the dead, but that this same Jesus Christ is present with His Church in the fullness of His love and grace 'even unto the end of the world'. Admittedly, the Christian Church has by no means always presented a very clear or convincing picture of divine love. Evils that can neither be denied nor excused have been done or tolerated by ecclesiastical authority in most branches of the Church; and there is the glaring scandal of division among Christians still. These things are a contradiction of the very gospel by which the Church lives. Nevertheless, wherever the Christian Church is found, there is the gospel in word and sacrament to tell the story of Jesus crucified and risen from the dead, and to testify to the divine love and grace that was incarnate in Him. It is true that the word can be preached, and the sacraments administered, in ways that obscure and distort the true nature of divine love; yet even so they are witnesses to its reality—and more than witnesses. Confronting us with the story of Jesus as a message of love addressed by God directly to us, they are vehicles and instruments through which the same divine love that was in action in Jesus is in action also with us.

That this is so, is attested by the fact that wherever the message of the gospel is believed, and in the measure in which it is believed, something of the Spirit of divine love is received and becomes an effective reality in the lives of those who believe. It is a quite evident and perceptible reality in the lives of the saints—and not in the famous and canonized saints only, but just as truly in those simple, humble Christian men and women in whom something of the same quality of love is seen that we have seen in Jesus Himself. They have received through His gospel the gift of His Spirit, and in and through them His love proves itself still a living reality, still a helping, healing, reconciling power. We have all—unless we have been either very unfortunate or very unobservant—met such people; and although we can, if we wish, explain it away, yet we know that they themselves attribute all that is good in them to the grace of our Lord Jesus Christ. They have been gripped by the grace and love which the gospel proclaims, and they are convinced that it comes from God Himself, the supreme and sovereign power in existence.

It has been this experience of grace that has most of all compelled the Christian Church from the beginning to insist that 'God was in Christ', that Christ was God incarnate. This is on the face of it an incredible assertion. How could God, the Almighty, the Infinite, the Eternal, submit to the limitations of a human life in time? Still worse, how could He possibly be crucified, dead, and buried? Or even if He could, is it conceivable that God, who is pure and perfect holiness and righteousness, would so forget His dignity, so defile Himself, as to descend to the level of friendship with sinful men? Well, if He could not, He would not be Almighty or Infinite, and if He would not, He would not be as good as Jesus, the best of men.

But the Incarnation of God does not mean, of course, that the activity of divine love is or ever was confined to a particular fraction of time and space, but only that in a particular fraction it has been revealed at its deepest and clearest. Those who have caught the Spirit of this revelation know very well how to trace the workings of divine love everywhere in the world and in their own lives, and where they cannot trace they confidently trust.

The Spirit of the God of love is actively present in judgement and grace wherever the gospel is proclaimed, and there are saints in every branch of the Christian Church. But in the Church, and even in the saints themselves, the Spirit of love is in conflict with other spirits, just as Jesus was involved in conflict in the days of His flesh. And just as Jesus seemed to have been defeated when He was crucified, so His Spirit sometimes seems to have been virtually extinguished. Yet in the history of the Church the Spirit has again and again manifested powers of renewal hardly less astonishing than the resurrection of Jesus from the dead. The Reformation of the sixteenth century and the Evangelical Revival of the eighteenth are outstanding examples of this in modern times. Reformations and revivals are in fact recurrent features of the life of the Church. They do not, it is true, recur with predictable regularity in a neat and tidy pattern, but it is not to be expected that they should. They are operations of the Spirit of the living God in His conflict with alien and hostile spiritual forces, and they are launched, not when we imagine the time is ripe, but when divine wisdom knows that it is.

If we are sometimes tempted to lose heart and despair of the state of the world and of the Church, or of our own lives, it is well to remember that we do not yet see the end of the work of God. We see and experience the confusion and tumult of conflicting forces, but not yet the outcome of the conflict; and there are undoubtedly times when it looks as though the powers of evil, the forces that make for destruction and death, would prevail. Nevertheless, we have a right to be sure that they will not. If we cannot see the shape of things to come, we can look back on the past and gain hope for the future from it. Above all, we can contemplate Jesus, crucified and risen from the dead, and find in Him the assurance that no situation can arise for us to face that is worse than He faced, and therefore none by which divine love can be baffled or defeated.

www.ingramcontent.com/pod-product-compliance
Lightning Source LLC
Chambersburg PA
CBHW050841160426
43192CB00011B/2109